PRAISE FOR *Solving the Student Loan Crisis*

This book tells you everything you always wanted to know about the nation's student debt crisis but were afraid to ask. It's a devastating indictment of our current system of financing higher education and makes it clear that only a complete transformation of how we pay for higher education in the U.S. can fix a very broken system.

—MORLEY WINOGRAD, President and Chief Enabling Officer, Campaign for Free College Tuition

An insightful and hard-hitting analysis of how a generation of students have and will be saddled with onerous debt in the United States. Combining the personal, historical, theoretical, and political in ways that are both illuminating and insightful, Johannsen casts a wide and necessary net in exploring the various ways in which debt has come to both indict and reveal a society in crisis, one that for all intent and purposes appears to no longer care about creating a secure future for its youth. A book that must be read, studied, and discussed if the juggernaut of debt and the stranglehold of the financial elite on democracy is to be challenged.

—HENRY GIROUX, McMaster University Professor for Scholarship in the Public Interest, Distinguished Visiting Professor at Ryerson University, and the Paulo Freire Distinguished Scholar in Critical Pedagogy

As an anti-debt veteran, Johannsen writes well about economic war. But her passionately argued book also takes us far into the dark side of student debt—depression, divorce, suicide—and then shows us a way out.

—ANDREW ROSS, Author of
Creditocracy and the Case for Debt Refusal

So much is said about the value of a college education. Johannsen uses personal experience and disturbing data to show readers a dark side of that education.

—JOHN HARNEY, Executive Editor,
The New England Journal of Higher Education

Solving the Student Loan Crisis

SOLVING
THE STUDENT LOAN
CRISIS

Dreams, Diplomas & A Lifetime of Debt

CRYN JOHANNSEN

NEW INSIGHTS
PRESS

Editorial Direction and Editing: Rick Benzel

Art Direction and Cover Design: Susan Shankin & Associates

Published by New Insights Press

New Insights Press is an imprint of the
Over And Above Creative Group
Los Angeles, CA

www.overandabovecreative.com

Publisher's Cataloging-In-Publication Data
(Prepared by The Donohue Group, Inc.)
Names: Johannsen, Cryn.

Title: Solving the student loan crisis : dreams, diplomas, and a lifetime of debt / Cryn Johannsen.

Description: First edition. | Los Angeles, CA : New Insights Press, an imprint of Change to Over And Above Creative Group, [2016] | Includes bibliographical references.

Identifiers: LCCN 2016902784 | ISBN 978-0-9965486-7-0 (print) | ISBN 978-0-9973357-0-5 (ebook)

Subjects: LCSH: Student loans--United States. | College graduates--United States--Finance, Personal. | College costs--United States. | Debt--United States.

Classification: LCC LB2340.2 .J64 2016 (print) | LCC LB2340.2 (ebook) | DDC 378.3/62/0973--dc23

First edition

Printed in the United States of America

Library of Congress Control Number: 2016902784

ISBN: 978-0-9965486-7-0

Visit Cryn's blog: alleducationmatters.blogspot.com

Contents

Acknowledgments

This book is dedicated to several supportive, caring, and loving people who believed in me. At many times they believed in me more than I believed in myself. One person in particular, I will name—Omar. I remember in the summer of 2015 when you told me that you were my biggest fan, and then told me to finish this book. Thank you for being there for me then. No matter where you are in the world, and despite our political disagreements, I know that you will always be rooting for me. I'll be doing the same for you. The others shall remain unnamed, but you know who you are, and to you, too, I am deeply indebted.

I'd also like to thank my editor, Rick Benzel, for his patience, strong critiques, and unfailing enthusiasm. The hours of rewrites he made me "endure" made this a truly viable and strong project—I am grateful for his support and guidance. In addition, I want to thank Susan Shankin, my visual designer, for doing such a superb job on the design of the book cover. It conveys the true possibilities we have, as conveyed in the content of my book, in solving the crisis for current debtors. On a final note, I also need to thank Morley Winograd. After all, if he hadn't introduced me to Rick, this project would have never come to fruition.

Introduction
Broken Bells in the Ivory Tower

I AM A PART OF THE INDENTURED EDUCATED CLASS, OWING A HUGE debt from loans I took out to get my diplomas.

I went to college between 1996 and 2001 to earn my B.A. degree. I then went to graduate school from 2001 to 2002 to earn an M.A. After that I was accepted into a PhD program and attended that from 2005 to 2007, earning another M.A. and completing a dissertation prospectus. While preparing for my qualifying exams, which are part of the requirements for many PhD programs, I took a leave of absence. Although I had plans to become an academic, it was after that time, in 2007, that I decided not to return.

Although I had received grants and scholarships from the schools I attended, the cost of these institutions far outweighed the assistance I received. I was forced to turn to loans of various sorts, including private bank loans. Several of my loans also had co-signers who agreed to help me. I entered the private sector shortly after I took a leave of absence, loaded down with all the loans I had taken out.

Today there are people with whom I no longer have any daily interactions, the most important being my ex-husband who was one of my co-signers, and yet we still have financial ties due to my student loans. Our marriage began breaking up several years ago, the weight of our financial problems due to my student loans dragging us into a tense relationship. Conflicts worsened when we found we could not make ends meet in Washington, DC where I began a new job after I left my PhD program. After a few years of struggling to pay bills in the DC area, the two of us decided to leave for Korea in 2010. I accepted a teaching job outside of Seoul, and my husband kept his job in the US while working virtually. I worked during the day in Korea as a teacher and he worked the graveyard shift in order to align his schedule with his office on the East Coast. Our apartment in Korea functioned much like a 24-hour running factory: someone was awake and working every hour of the day, because of our work schedules.

If our financial situation had been different, I am not certain we would have made that decision to cross the Pacific. But one of the reasons we chose to "flee" our home in the US were my student loans. We had an unconscious sense that by going to Korea, we might overcome the student loan debt. Perhaps by earning more money in Korea, and enjoying a much lower cost of living there, we could pay off a big chunk of the student loans I owed to the lenders. That was our hope anyway.

We spent about a year in Korea, and returned to the US because we realized that we wanted to live in our homeland. But the stress of paying my student loans eventually got the best of us. Our marriage deteriorated into constant battles over how much I owed and how we could possibly pay it. Despite years of paying some of it off, I still owed a staggering amount of money because I had chosen a path to become an academic and teach.

When any marriage disintegrates, particularly one that lasted nearly ten years, there are a multitude of reasons. Many of the reasons are never fully understood by either partner, yet they cause things to implode. But I can say with absolute certainty that my student loan debt played a significant role in the demise of my marriage. Love and understanding were replaced with simmering, sometimes violent resentment over the money I owed. The best solution was to part ways.

My student loan debt has taken a toll on my emotional health and my general outlook on life. I try my hardest to hide this from others, especially those closest to me, but some days it just comes out, the hopelessness, the fear that I will wind up destitute and homeless. All of these overwhelming insecurities haunt me. There are days in which my outstanding student loan debt gets the best of me. Indeed, the possibility of impending financial doom hangs above me like the sword of Damocles.

About six years ago, when I was still optimistic about our political process to deal with the rising crisis of student loan debt, I made a decision to do something about my predicament. I decided to turn my personal story and my plight into a political and intellectual project in order to fight on behalf of the millions of other students and borrowers like me suffering from loan debt in the US. With my background in history, especially the history of social and political movements, I launched a website about student loan debt. Called *All Education Matters* (alleducationmatters.blogspot.com), I began exploring *all* things relating to this topic. My blog was among the first to map this issue out as a national American crisis. When I first began writing, no one else was making a peep about it.

My biggest focus in the beginning was to share testimonials from people who, like me, were members of the indentured educated class. All Education Matters was a safe place for those with student loan debt to share their life stories about their insecurities, their fears, and anything that transpired to them because of their debt.

Little by little, I began delving into why so many millions of students had such serious debt. Who was responsible for creating this crisis? Why was it burgeoning out of control? What could be done about having millions of students graduate college owing tens of thousands of dollars, if not more than $100,000 before they even had a job?

This is when I discovered that our student loan debt problem was enormously complex. Just like any crisis of this magnitude, there is no single cause and it is difficult to point a finger at any one person as responsible. There are a number of players and institutions involved and they played a clear role. It was a case of a perfect storm of factors that came together to create a massive system aimed to take advantage of students seeking higher education. The biggest players are: the federal government (politicians on *both* sides of the aisle as well as the Department of Education), the loan lenders (who are totally unregulated), and the universities (both the for-profits *and* non-profits). Together, they form an enormous industry that I call "Higher Ed Inc." that has turned millions of students into long-term debtors.

In my research, I examined how student loans were bought and sold on Wall Street. I exhaustively investigated all aspects of how the money was allocated, who was making a profit off of these loans, and how it was hurting student borrowers and their families. I thought about the implications of this problem on our society as I watched the crisis get bigger and bigger. If you are not aware of how large the student loan debt problem has become, let me break it to you not so gently:

Today, the student loan debt crisis has mushroomed into a national crisis, with 43 million Americans in debt for having gone to college. Their total debt is a whopping $1.3 trillion dollars. That's roughly 1 in 8 Americans that owes money for getting a higher education and trying to better himself or herself. And nearly every one of those people has a parent, a spouse, a loved one, a friend, or a co-signer who is also affected by this problem. I might venture to guess that as much as 1 in 6 Americans is impacted in some way by the student loan debt crisis.

The student loan debt crisis is now part of our national vocabulary, covered in newspapers on nearly a daily basis. While the topic has been popular in terms of how to tackle "personal debt" on an individual-by-individual basis, and countless books are available that focus on solving one's own student loan debt, this book stands apart from those titles because I demonstrate how this is a collective US catastrophe. All of our stories, reflecting the millions of us who are indebted, are part of a national narrative that has created this crisis. Books on finding "free college money," going to school for "free," "getting out of debt quick," and so forth actually do a disservice to the complexities and manipulations that have created this crisis and allow it to worsen with each graduating class. It is now a topic that all the presidential candidates are discussing as a key issue for the 2016 election. Candidates as far apart on most issues like former Republican Marco Rubio and Independent / Democrat Bernie Sanders both agree on at least the concept that something must be done to solve the crisis. There are numerous bills in Congress proposing solutions, but little consensus as to which one to support.

This book is dedicated to the millions of student loan debtors, parents, friends of students, and others who deserve a voice in a system that has failed them. At the end of this book, I synthesize seven possible solutions as follows, and discuss their pros and cons:

- Implement a debt jubilee in which all debt is forgiven
- Offer free public universities
- Enable debtors to refinance loans at lower interest rates
- Make IBR (Income Based Repayment) after forgiveness of 20 years non-taxable and bill-free
- Reestablish bankruptcy protection rights for borrowers
- Tackle the crisis at the *state* level, aiding prospective students, current students, and distressed borrowers
- Actively support politicians who fight on behalf of student borrowers

Whichever of these solutions appeals to you, I hope this book will motivate everyone, whether you are a policymaker, government official, past debtor, co-signer, current student on assistance, parent of a current debtor, future student, or future parent of a student to join me in making our voices heard.

It's time to change this crazy paradigm we have of educating Americans while destroying their dreams by putting them in debt for decades, if not an entire lifetime. This entire country deserves better in the way we educate our people to be intelligent, productive, thoughtful, and gainfully-employed citizens.

FINAL NOTE: Some may wonder why I have not disclosed the total amount of student loan debt I still owe. There are several reasons for why I have chosen not to do so. For starters, I have always made it clear that I am quite indebted, just like many of the people who have sent me their testimonials. I decided that fully disclosing my own amount would only detract from the goals I have to raise awareness about this being a *collective crisis*. Working on this project is not about me and my debt, but instead about how it is hurting millions of Americans and the health of this country. In order to stay focused on being of service to those I represent, I decided it was in the best interest of all to not disclose my total amount of debt owed. For those who are enemies of this movement, of which there are many, one can easily imagine the remarks that would be hurled at me. I would be quickly dismissed as wanting to "solve" the crisis for my own personal gain, when that is far from the truth. On the flip side, those suffering from debt might perceive my debt as being inconsequential compared to theirs. Thus, these are the reasons why I have determined not to disclose what I still owe.

Chapter 1
A Bleak Future
for America

A COLOSSAL FAILURE OF POLITICAL AND SOCIAL VISION is upon us. Thanks to the creation of "Higher Ed Inc.," we now live in a dystopian country with millions of educated Americans struggling to pay or completely unable to pay their student loan debts. Try as they might—power brokers, politicians, and bankers who have wittingly or unwittingly created this crisis cannot escape what they have created for all of us.

The health of this country and its future are in peril. And if we do not reverse this dystopic situation, which has been shamefully devised by profiteers who are part of the student lending industry, one in which the red badge of debt has been invisibly written across our foreheads and occupies our thoughts, we as a nation face a bleak future with many political, economic, and social ramifications in the future.

Having studied the student debt loan problem for nearly ten years, let me paint a picture of the consequences if we do not change the way America educates our citizens at the university level and beyond.

Substantial brain drain

First, we will have significant brain drain, something that is already occurring, as our own students, our best and brightest, will depart to other countries for their education, where they often remain for their first jobs. Brain drain is a serious problem in nations where it occurs. We've seen the impact that the massive loss of the educated class—teachers, scientists, doctors, and other professionals—has done in countries like Russia, India, Peru and elsewhere, where millions of highly educated people have left. Recently, Presidential candidate Bernie Sanders wrote an op-ed for the *Washington Post*, arguing several points for why the US needs free public education. In his op-ed, he mentioned the fact that over 4,600 American students leave the US to attend German institutions of higher learning alone. Think of how many other countries are now educating young Americans.

Many young people have started to leave the country for better job opportunities elsewhere, in part to escape their loan debt or to have a better chance at continuing their higher education at less expense. There have been many readers who have come to *All Education Matters*—my website devoted to this topic—and have shared their stories about fleeing the US and leaving permanently. It doesn't take a rocket scientist to know that the best and brightest of our country realize they can leave for countries such as Germany and receive the same level of education for free.

In the summer of 2015, one debtor wrote on my website about his decision to flee the country:

I am a US expat who is a 'student loan debt fugitive.' There are many of us here in the EU [. . .] I am living outside the country with US student debt. I won't bore you all with my story, but the end game is I cannot possibly pay it back. Even if I were to enter IBR *[the US government loan forgiveness program]*, the amount forgiven would be equal to hitting the lottery and having to pay taxes on that amount would be insurmountable. In my not always humble opinion, IBR is a political scam to basically kick the can down the road without actually forgiving debt. What it does is turn a civil debt into a criminal tax liability.

Anyway, it is pretty obvious I am in default. I graduated 3 years ago and my monthly net pay was not going to pay my medical school loan. I attempted to contact my creditors and work out a plan and both the federal and private lenders basically told me I could get short-term relief, but there was no solution for more than a year. They also straight out told me they had absolutely no incentive to negotiate because 'they would get their money one way or another.'

The country I am in does discharge student loans in bankruptcy. In fact, a judge can declare you bankrupt on the spot [my emphasis].

My estimated monthly student loan payment is more than 3 times a doctor's gross salary here.

No court here would accept the amounts and penalties the US imposes. In fact, the law here has its own ideas about what is an acceptable penalty and they do not include collection or attorney fees. The interest is modest at 6%. So when my creditors called I simply said 'sue me!' (I may have mentioned that any lawsuit must be in the native language and filled out in the requirements of the local law.) The reality is nobody in their right mind from the US would sue me here. They would pay enormous fees for translation and local legal aid, to watch me be declared insolvent on the first court appearance. The statute of limitations for suing over debt here is 3 years anyway, so in a few months I could just claim that.

I actually encourage people, if you can't pay your US student loans, pack up and move. I think it is foolish not to. Sometimes I feel bad about not being able to pay the money back, but I suspect just like homesickness, it will fade with time.

Chances are high that many more student loan debtors will opt to flee the US and find countries that will treat them more favorably. Why would any of them want to move back to the US when its laws are so punitive against student loan debtors, especially those who default when they simply cannot pay? Why are these laws written in favor of the lenders? As anyone with student loan debt is aware, lenders have unbelievable power and leverage against borrowers in this country.

But there is another type of brain drain occurring within US borders—the loss of critical thinking skills among the adult populace, skills that are necessary in a highly technological and sophisticated culture. It results in a gap in a basic and shared understanding of how government functions and how it ought to function for the common good. An educated populace who understands civics and how democratic institutions work is reflected in the set of beliefs they espouse and the leaders they choose.

Our bias against free or low-cost higher education reflects a myopic cultural trend that exists widely in America — anti-intellectualism, which has a long history in the US, and has intensified in recent years. One only need to look at demagogues like Sarah Palin and Donald Trump, among others, as evidence that the US contains millions of people who blame intellectuals for misguiding the country. It is well-known that this anti-intellectualism in America fuels a growth of crazy conspiracy theories about many events and causes, as well as a broad cultural paranoia about progress. Donald Trump's populist rallies illustrate how political leaders can feed into this type of dangerous thinking. Trump himself has been accused by individuals — public intellectuals on both the right and the left — of being a fascist, and preying and exploiting a sort of anti-intellectualism that fuels racism, hatred, xenophobia and other forms of irrational thinking among significant portions of the population.

On the other hand, an educated citizenry is, it would seem, more resistant to such anti-intellectualism. They are less prone to accept arguments based on xenophobia, shortsighted calls that appeal to dumbed-down nationalism, and pat answers that are simply illogical. Indeed, Karl Rove asserted once that to win, Republicans must run an election on "Guns, God, and gays." That sentiment has become uglier, as Donald Trump's presidential run in 2016 reveals the many disconcerting sociopathic and fascistic tendencies in populist American culture.

This is where higher education comes into play, and how it is a crucial lifeline in a democratic society to provide people with education that helps develop critical thinking skills, an open mind, and a respect for learning.

Psychological problems, personal loss, and broken dreams

A second consequence of our system of financing higher education is a tremendous dark cloud hanging over America's youth, who more than any other generation are so in debt that they cannot move forward with their lives. The graduating class of 2015 were the most indebted to ever receive diplomas. Unable to find jobs to meet their monthly student loan repayments, they move back home or double up with roommates. In 2012, it was estimated that 85% of college graduates moved back home to live with their parents. Many young people are unable to buy cars, homes, or start families. Clearly, this is a drag on the economy, but few speak of the psychological toll this is taking on young people who want and are expected to graduate from school, land a good paying job, and make it on their own. After all, that is what has been happening for several generations. This is the mindset of young people who go to college, expecting it to be the path to their American dream.

The sense of personal failure for many young folks is tremendous, as the testimonials I have received indicate. There is also a sense of deep isolation related to the debt that they have acquired, especially when there is the perception that it was a bad choice of their own making. This claim reinforces a lot of guilt in young people, when in fact, it is a principal of our culture that going to college matters. High school seniors usually believe that it makes sense to get a higher degree, and this "meme" that a college degree is essentially a ticket to success is constantly reinforced by our leading figures (politicians, college Presidents, celebrities, etc.)

The "financialization" of debt in the United States is particularly dangerous to the ideals of the American Dream, understood as the ability to move up the socioeconomic ladder, particularly when pursuing a degree in higher education. The mantra of going to university to better oneself has been recited—for good reasons—for generations. But now the cost is solely on the shoulders of borrowers and the parents (or other respective co-signers).

Financial aid today is a misleading term, as it is really more about buying credit that will have to be repaid at a higher cost in the future. Furthermore, it is so-called credit that is managed not only recklessly but immorally. Instead of higher education being a sound investment that will help graduates earn higher wages in the labor market, the current way in which it is financed should actually be considered a regressive tax. Professor Robert Meister at the University of California at Santa Cruz put it this way, "Student loans are the largest remaining form of subprime credit. If they weren't subprime, you wouldn't call them financial aid."

When I first began writing about the student loan debt debacle around 2010, there were only a handful of articles that discussed student loan debt. Most of these were written by various experts, most notably Sandy Baum, who claimed student loan debt was "good debt." Baum, in fact, to my knowledge, still makes this assertion.

Americans struggling with student loan debt both financially and psychologically would beg to differ with Baum, as the testimonials that I have collected over the past years attest. Baum and others, to my knowledge, never discuss the real life repercussions of student loan debt, such as depression, familial and relationship travails when they sit on panels in DC or elsewhere pontificating on the topic. Using anachronistic rhetoric more appropriate to the 1980s, policy wonks like her continue to insist that higher education is a "good investment." They conveniently omit or downplay the fact that students and families might carry a burden of $20,000, $50,000 or even $100,000 after "investing" in college. With one false "move"—a death, a health problem, a lost job, a broken marriage—borrowers and co-signers find themselves in an economic tailspin that can quickly accelerate at warp speed towards financial ruin.

Colleges and universities don't have to worry about this type of personal and financial ruin, as they have already been paid from the revenues they receive from the federal government which were disbursed while the student was enrolled at their institution. Meanwhile, the federal government ensures that it collects on unpaid debts. This describes a good part of the machinery behind "Higher Ed Inc."

The darkest side of student debt

There is an even more serious and sadder side to the student loan debt crisis than the brain drain. We now face a mental health emergency in which many young people in debt are contemplating suicide. This part of the issue, the shocking effects that the student loan debt crisis are having on mental health, cannot be overlooked or forgotten. While researching this book, I discovered that loan debt is a cause of suicide among young people and is a mental health emergency.

On August 17, 2010, I put out a question on my blog, asking for people to reply. In my column called "Suicide Among Student Debtors—Who's Thought About it?" I asked people to send me their stories. My question read as follows:

> There are quite a number of articles about the concern that suicide rates will increase vis-a-vis the increased number of people who are facing long-term unemployment *(here's the*

most recent one I've come across). But what about those who are struggling to pay their student loans? Here are several more personal questions I have about this highly sensitive topic:

○ Have you contemplated suicide because of the amount of student loan debt you owe?

○ Have you started engaging in risky behavior (heavy drinking, using drugs, etc.) because of your student loan debt?

○ Are you taking medications, such as anti-anxiety pills or anti-depressants, to cope with being an indentured educated citizen?

The responses I received were overwhelming. Even today, years after I posted these questions, individuals continue to write me about their suicidal thoughts. Here are some of the saddest letters and emails I've received:

It crosses my mind daily. Then I realize my mom co-signed two of my loans and they will be knocking on her door after I'm dead and gone. I've realized my life is ruined because of these loans. If Sallie Mae, Chase, Citi, Firstmark, etc. would accept the $50 I could afford to send them, I wouldn't be in the despair I am in.

Another person wrote:

I fully intend to kill myself the moment I finish my PhD, which will be in 8-9 months. I was lucky enough to receive full funding for my doctoral program, but carry a great deal of debt from undergrad. I realize now that a PhD in humanities guarantees me a life of miserable poverty and debt-related harassment. That, combined with the scorn I know

I will face from more successful family members makes life unappealing. I would do it now, but for some reason I'm still invested in finishing my thesis. Not long to wait, in any case.

One writer told me that fellow law grads were talking about committing murder-suicides:

Law grad here. I've got several lawyer friends with similar debt levels who are nearing the end of their ropes. Of those who've admitted to contemplating suicide, I'm surprised by the number who've told me that if they go out, they have no intention of going alone. If they're telling the truth (and I hope to god they're not), I certainly would not want to be a law school administrator.

As a result of these responses I continued to explore and do follow ups, one of which was this post [it's truncated]:

So many people are hurting, and so many people are thinking about killing themselves. These people aren't crazy. Far from it. They are approaching their indebtedness from a rational perspective, and sadly suicide seems like a viable choice. That's not out of the norm. When there are severe economic downturns, people often turn to drastic measures to get out of a hopeless predicament. Financial ruin leads many healthy people to an early grave, and quite often it's from their own hand. As Barbara Ehrenreich stated quite frankly in an article from 2008 entitled, 'Suicide Spreads as One Solution to the Debt Crisis,' when people feel backed up against a wall, it's only natural for them to say, 'Just shoot me!' At that time, many people who found their homes being repossessed chose to proclaim, 'I'll just shoot myself!'

After listening to a radio interview I did on NPR about the topic of suicide, and the specific article I wrote about it for *The Economic Hardship and Reporting Project,* with authors Barbara Ehrenreich and Gary Rivlin as my editors, a reader let me know that she/he contemplated jumping from the 27th floor of a work building *every day.* These stories continued to flood in to my web site about suicidal ideation. Here's what the one who thought about jumping wrote:

Cryn, I listened to your interview and cried for hours. I graduated from law school with honors back in 2003 and never found a job as an attorney. I've worked a bunch of odd jobs the last 7 years just to survive. I've been a retail worker, a call center worker, a housekeeper, a dishwasher, and a temp–seriously, it seems like I've been everything except what I went to school for! I know my life is ruined and that I will never be a practicing attorney. I get it, really I do. After all, I'm around attorneys 24/7 in my current job and they look down their noses at me or else just ignore me. I am a loser and no one wants to be around a loser or else they might become one too.

I try to remind myself that my life wasn't always like this–that people used to like me and that I had a lot going for me in college and even law school. However, after years of being snubbed and treated so terribly, I have learned to be as invisible as possible and to keep to myself. I'm sure that gives everyone at work a good laugh–then they can say I'm anti-social or not good with people and therefore not attorney material.

I could live without being a practicing attorney but what I can't get over is the fact I ruined my life by borrowing

$100,000 to go to law school. I thought I was making a really good investment in myself because I believed in myself back then. I knew I would do well in school, and I guess I thought I would get a job and be able to pay back my loans. How incredibly wrong I turned out to be. Even if I am able to get out of student loan debt, I will be starting over from scratch. Zero savings. Zero retirement. Zero career options.

Every day I think about jumping out the 27th floor window of the office building where I am currently working to escape the mess I have made of my life. I am in so deep now, there is no way out. I used to keep myself up at night thinking about how I would ever pay my student loans off, but now I keep myself up at night, wondering if this is really how the next 30 years of my life will be — always moving from one dead-end job to the next [...]

I'm sorry this is long and depressing, but it's nice to get this all out. I am not asking anyone to forgive my student loans; I fully intend to pay back every last cent I borrowed. I just want to feel like all of my hard work and sacrifice was worth it, instead of always feeling humiliated, embarrassed, ashamed, bitter and angry. I'm so tired of feeling this way — I just want the pain to go away. Thanks for listening.

It didn't stop there. Student loan debtors continued reporting to me stories of suicidal ideation in relation to their student loan debt. Furthermore, since the original story, sponsored by the *Economic Hardship and Reporting Project*, was an immediate success, I wound up being interviewed by more media outlets.

Luckily, there were also debtors who told me that my voice saved their life. One man wrote me and said:

Hi, I came across a website tonight that talked about student loan debt and suicide. I am a military veteran and also a person who completed a master's degree in 2012. Since getting my masters *[sic]* degree, I have really struggled with many things. Some of my struggles are related to PTSD from my military service in Iraq but I have found recently my real stress comes from not being able to find a job that pays me a wage that will empower. Furthermore, I have been divorced since I came back from Iraq, I was not the same person who went over there. I have been unstable with jobs since then and the jobs I did have I have not been able to make a decent living as I have been in and out of homelessness. In fact, I am writing this email while lying on the floor in the living room of my ex-wife's house. :-(

I write this email to you just to say I enjoyed reading your post on that website about student loan debt and suicide. I think about suicide given my situation. I feel I have nothing anymore and no one loves me. I am alone every day in my thoughts and physically. I often feel hopeless, but yet have so many dreams and desires about the career I want to work in after having received my masters *[sic]* degree . . . .

I do not know why I am really sending this email to you. I guess because you mentioned in the comment section to another person who was thinking of suicide that they could email you to discuss things or their thoughts. You seem like a real supportive person and I liked reading your post on that website.

I do not know if you will even get this email since the post I was reading from you were from back in 2011. I hope my email finds you well. I wish I knew you and had you as a friend. In your written words you seem very understanding

13

and have desire to help. For this, I want to keep pushing forward and not end my life . . . . However, the pain I have and
the depression are still there. Thank you for being there.

I wrote him back immediately and urged him to reach
out to people he trusted—friends or family—to talk to them
about his suicidal feelings. I also told him to seek medical help
from either a psychiatrist or a therapist. I requested that he
write me back the next day to provide me with an update. The
man did write me back, and he did exactly as I had advised.
He is on a better path now, a much better path, and is no longer suicidal. In fact, he is thriving.

If only I had had the reach to save another particular student loan debtor, however. In late May of 2015, I received an
email that I had hoped to never receive. It was from a man
I will call Bob.[1] The worst of tragedies had struck his family
only a few days before reaching out to me. He wrote:

> My name is Bob, I live in the Upper Ohio River Valley area,
> which is notorious for its's [sic] economic ups & downs.
> Families fight & work hard for what little they have, and it's
> tough to get by. Fortunately for myself, I am not in a large
> amount of debt. But only for one reason . . . I did not go to
> college for longer than one semester. I quit school, worked
> as much as possible & eventually ended up working in a coal
> mine. I make a good living, have a wonderful home, fantas-
> tic wife & a beautiful daughter. All because I avoided school
> to go underground & play with rocks for the past 10 years.
> (Although, I was laid off 2 weeks ago, and find out my fate
> tomorrow morning on if I go back to work or not.)
>
> I wish that I could say the same for the rest of my fam-
> ily. My mother is 70 years old, buried under stress & paper

work, while she tries to care for my father, who suffers from Alzheimer's type dementia & now 'lives' in a nursing home. I call it 'living' because it is more like existing until death. My oldest sister, who is 38, lives at home with my mother too. She had some learning disabilities when she was younger, and this placed her in some special education classes, which she did not need to be in, and held her back from learning properly. She in turn helps me by taking care of my mom & visiting with her at the nursing home with my dad.

Our second sister lives in England, she is 7 months pregnant & has a fantastic husband. She is in debt to Navient for $88,000 in private loans. And this is least of our problems, because she is making what they say is the required monthly payment (for now, who knows what trick they will pull on her later).

And now the reason I am writing this letter in the first place. I was searching online about the connections between student loans & suicide when I came across your article: 'The Ones We've Lost: The Student Loan Debt Suicides' on the Huffington Post from July 2, 2012. With the heaviest of hearts, I have to say that my brother-in-law, [*name redacted*] committed suicide on May 12, 2015 (last Tuesday). He was my brother, I loved him dearly. My sister came home to find him & now I am in-constant worry of her mental state too. [My brother-in-law] had a large amount of private loans being handled by Navient, of which I have yet to get the final number on. He was in his second year of medical school at [*University name redacted*]. My sister, now in her second year of doctor residency in the surgery department at [*University name redacted*], also has at least $135,000 in debt owed to Navient.

I know that not one issue can fully be blamed for my brother (in-law)'s suicide, but I do know for a fact that the student loans were the main driving force. We now have a GoFundMe campaign running in his honor to try to help my sister deal with all of the associated costs of this tragedy (I.E.–funeral home expenses, memorial, cremation, the crime scene cleanup bill, hopefully her moving from their home, and hopefully relocating/finding a new hospital to work at that doesn't force her into 80 to 120-hour work weeks).

Navient has cost my family money, stress, tears, fights, screaming matches, and now, unimaginable heartache as we mourn [him]. My mother receives upwards of 30 calls per day (every day) at home, telling her that her house will be taken away, her car will be repossessed, and that my father will be kicked out of the nursing home if she doesn't get the loans paid up that my parents cosigned for as my dad was in failing health. We don't know what to do. We don't know where to go. I am sure that you receive many letters & phone calls that sound just the same as we do in our situation, and I have to say that I am extremely grateful that you have even read this far as I know I have rambled on too long.

My point is, we are lost, we are scared. I miss my brother (in law) with all of my heart. I lost all of the dreams of us sharing life together & being hiking buddies on the Appalachian Trail. My sister lost her love, my daughter lost her uncle. I don't want to lose any more. I want to fight. Please tell me or help me in our fight. We don't know what to do. My mother is scared that she will die with these debts. My parent's [sic] credit is ruined, so are my sister's [sic]. Mine is still good, but I am afraid that one day, these debts will fall on me, and ruin the life I am trying to build with my wife & daughter. We've decided since his death, we won't be having any more kids. The world of debt & what it brings with it scares us too much.

Please, can you help point us in a direction out of this? Or is there a way out? Is this something that needs to be handled by politicians? I hope not, because we'll all be long gone before that happens.

Thank you for your time. I know this was long & rambling. I promise you, I am not crazy. I am just stressed, and at a loss of what to do, and in mourning. Your article and **ALL EDUCATION MATTERS** are an inspiration. Please keep fighting the fight.

Bob (and family)

Several years ago, I spoke by phone with Peter Kinderman about mental health and student loan debt. Kinderman is Professor of Clinical Psychology at the University of Liverpool, and President-Elect of the British Psychological Society. Pieces of that telephone conversation were included in my original article about student loans and suicide. I followed up with him for additional thoughts about this issue, and I let him know about this recent suicide. In a reply email, Kinderman wrote me:

We know that social factors are fundamentally important contributors to our mental health and wellbeing. This, of course, means that economic factors—employment, unemployment, and debt—are hugely important. We know that, since the 2008 economic recession, there have been a range of serious mental health problems linked directly to unemployment, job insecurity, and financial difficulties. Mental health problems, even suicide, are known consequences of economic difficulties.

In other words, these stories I am reporting are not due to bizarre, inexplicable, illnesses. These are the normal, natural—but terrible—consequences of people finding themselves in grave financial difficulty. The stories essentially tell themselves—people worried sick on a daily basis about how to meet their everyday living expenses, how to repay their loans, and how to rebuild their lives and businesses.

When an individual man or woman is in seemingly inescapable financial difficulties, when there seems to be no way out, it's not surprising that he or she becomes anxious, depressed, hopeless. These emotions are perhaps particularly difficult if, as in the case of student debt, the initial debts were incurred as result of a personal decision, the choice to get higher education. The paradox is that the choice to study at university is universally regarded as wise and sensible, and loans to support education are almost always regarded as appropriate—they are even supported by governments in many countries, but not in America.

Comments on my original post have continued to come in to me. In August of 2015, one individual wrote:

> I am planning on killing myself because of my student debt. I owe over 70K and don't even have an undergraduate degree to show for it — I maxed out on government subsidized loans and cannot take out private loans because I had to file for bankruptcy. I'm 10 classes short of my bachelor's degree but have no way to pay for it. So that 70K in debt that I have is all for nothing. Trying to get a college degree was THE worst mistake of my life, and I have no one to blame but myself. Nonetheless, I cannot agree to a lifetime of debt slavery.

I've taken out a life insurance policy to at least leave some money behind for my family. Thankfully, I live in a state that has a law which requires all insurance companies to pay the full death benefit even in cases of suicide, as long as the policy has been in effect for one year. I have a complete plan in place, and my intention is to do it in such a way that my organs are viable for donation. I hope and pray that I manage to pull it off so that my life wasn't a complete waste.

In my view, several serious questions remain: how many more suicidal debtors are there, and how many others have actually gone through with either attempting to commit suicide or have successfully done it? How many innocent lives has student loan debt taken?

Jeopardizing our economy and national security

From a strategic perspective, the student loan debt crisis is also a serious economic problem for the US and could even impact our national security. In a 2015 National Security Strategy report, President Barack Obama argued, "Our higher education system is the finest in the world, drawing more of the best students globally every year." On the surface, this may appear to be true, but there remains an issue of concern that I suggest must be considered. It is a significant economic benefit to America that our institutions of higher education attract the best students globally every year, but if a large number of them become permanent debtors every year, the ones especially who will stay in the US job market upon graduating, how does that offer us an economic edge? The short answer is: It doesn't. There are several reasons why.

First, student loan debt will block the path to professional success for many of those "best and brightest," and their debt affects every aspect of our society. As mentioned, many young professionals with college or university degrees simply leave the country, as some are already choosing to do now. Their departure undermines our technological edge, a key determinant in any country's competitiveness today.

There is also a sizeable economic loss to the income of student debtors. In August of 2013, Demos, a think tank based in New York, published a study, "At What Cost? How Student Debt Reduces Lifetime Wealth," in which they wrote, "Our model finds that an average student debt burden for a dual-headed household with bachelors' degrees from 4-year universities ($53,000) leads to a lifetime wealth loss of nearly $208,000." So, instead of the common argument that earning a degree means that an individual will earn more money over his or her lifetime, this study suggests that many graduates experience a huge drop in lifetime earnings. Losing over $200,000 is the equivalent of three full years of a $70,000 salary—as if you had worked all those years for absolutely nothing. If you calculate that after-tax income it takes to make up a loss of $210,000, it's probably more like losing close to four years of one's income.

Several Federal Reserve studies[2] have recently debated how serious the current student loan situation is. One study in 2012 by the Federal Reserve Bank of Kansas City presented statistics about student loan debt burdens and delinquency rates, and discussed the concerns among many Americans about the fiscal impact of student loans. The message in this report confirmed that student loans presented problems for *some* borrowers, but it concluded that those problems, while worth addressing, did not yet impose a significant financial burden on society.

However, in a New York Federal Reserve Bank report published in 2013, an opposite assessment of the burden to America was the message. This report noted that "[s]tudent loan debt is the only form of consumer debt that has grown since the peak of consumer debt in 2008. Balances of student loans have eclipsed both auto loans and credit cards, making student loan debt the largest form of consumer debt outside of mortgages." If we read between the lines here, it suggests that student loan debt makes it difficult for student debtors, and there are 43 million of us, to buy homes and automobiles, two key elements that help spur economic growth in a consumer-driven economy.

The New York Federal Reserve's desire to measure the size of the student loan debt load also says a lot about how concerned the central bank is about a possible threat to the economy. "Our job is to really understand what's happening in the financial system," and the "very rapid rise in student loan debt over the last few years [can] actually have some pretty significant consequences to the economic outlook," President William Dudley told reporters in November of 2014.

By 2015, top economists such as Joseph Stiglitz and Paul Krugman, both Nobel Prize winners, were warning about the student loan debt crisis and how it affects major life decisions for people in the United States. In an interview with the magazine *Attn.*, Stiglitz noted, "In the American model [of higher education], the debt is so large and payments are so high that it is really affecting important life choices that young people are facing. It means they can't get married, it means they can't buy a house, it means someone who goes to law school feels like he has to go into corporate law [in order to get a high salary that will allow him/her to pay off their loan]."

Krugman has many times offered a similar critique. As early as 2012, when interviewed by PBS, he explained, "the preponderance of the evidence is that the biggest single factor keeping us where we are, keeping us in this depression, is the overhang of debt." When the interviewer asked more specifically about student loan debt, Krugman replied, "Household debt is the big ball and chain on this economy, and student debt is a big part of it." Later, when Krugman was interviewed by Princeton Magazine[3] shortly before he retired in 2015 to join the faculty at Graduate Center, City University of New York, he was asked, "Do you have any concern that mounting student loan debt will eventually impact the economy and housing market?" to which he replied, "It's already happening. Household formation is very low, and debt has to be part of the explanation."

These macro explanations from top economists match my own findings from the hundreds of testimonials I have received from student debtors who have told me that they are unable to buy homes, purchase cars, start families, launch businesses—all because of the fact that they are weighed down by their student loans. Again, this is a direct result of the machinery that makes "Higher Ed Inc." function.

A bleak future

The prognosis for our country is bleak if we fail to fix the problem of how past debtors with $40,000, $50,000, or even $100,000 of loans can pay off their loans, as well as how we can help millions of young Americans in college now or about to enter a school of higher education pay for their educations.

Should fewer students see the value of getting a B.A., M.A., or other degree, we will become increasingly ignorant and incapable of solving the pressing issues that our society now faces. If fewer young people and even working adults who want to go back to school have to pass up attending institutions of higher education just to avoid massive student loan debt, the collective loss of knowledge and critical thinking skills will doom this country. Just as no city wants to accept a population consisting of only high school graduates (or dropouts), it seems obvious that our entire country would not want the majority of our population to consist of people who have only a high school or A.A. degree.

The question is: *Are we too late or can we redeem ourselves?*

Chapter 2
A Brief History of US Investment in Higher Education

MANY AMERICANS ARE NOT AWARE THAT STUDENT loans and student loan debt didn't always exist. For decades, public colleges in states such as California and New York were either free or charged nominal fees. In other states, the cost of higher education at a state university was quite reasonable. Such free access or low cost of tuition, however, began to change around the time President Ronald Reagan took office. Since then, costs of higher education have skyrocketed to the point that they provide worse sticker shock than buying a new car for most families.

Let's face it, not only is the cost of college education no longer free, it is simply no longer even affordable for the majority of Americans. Over the last 34 years, the cost of college has increased by more than 1100%.[4] This situation has been prompted by multiple causes: rising fees that most colleges charge, the lack of governmental over-sight, and profit-driven models of capitalism poorly applied to higher education. All of these factors have led directly to the formation of industries that are involved in the "financializa-tion" of educational debt. Rather than having a system focused on educating America's youth at a reasonable cost, we have a system that effectively serves only one purpose: to enrich those who run the companies that rely on the indenture of millions of Americans who want to get a higher education. And that is precisely how "Higher Education Inc." has been designed to operate, or at least its more recent iterations.

As mentioned, outstanding student loan debt now stands at $1.3 trillion, a figure that surpasses the credit card debt and auto loans of Americans. (By the time this book is pub-lished and you read this, it will likely be even higher.) The only other debt larger than student loan debt is mortgage debt, and the difference between these two forms of debt is that the borrower gets an actual physical item in exchange for the latter debt: property. With student loan debt, more and more students have nothing or little to show for it. They either don't graduate, succumbing to the weight of their current debt and fear of taking on more debt just to finish their degree. Or they do graduate yet have difficulty finding a job quickly that provides a decent enough salary to repay their loans within a reasonable period of time, not a lifetime.

In 2012, according to The Institute for College Access and Success (TICAS.org), 71% of all students graduating from four-year colleges had student loan debt. That represents 1.3 million students graduating with debt, up from 1.1 million in 2008 and 0.9 million in 2004.[5] That figure is a dramatic change from the 1990s, when many students did not take out loans to go to school. There is no doubt that costs are escalating. The graduating class of 2015 became the most indebted to receive diplomas, and it is likely that each coming year, a new winner of debt will take over.[6]

Students aren't the only borrowers either. One in ten parents also borrow on their student's behalf,[7] whether by co-signing on private loans (according to a Consumer Financial Protection Bureau (CFPB) study, 90% of all private loans require a co-signer[8]) or by taking out their own loans on behalf of their student via the Parent PLUS Loan program (these are loans which can never be legally taken over by the student, so the parent is on the hook). Both of these options are dangerous and ensnare another generation of people within families to a lifetime of owing student loan debt.

The entire setup of co-signers needing to get involved has become a "debt trap" for parents. It poses a serious threat to them becoming responsible for repaying the loans in the event of unforeseen calamitous events that could occur in the student's lifetime. Worse, it can lead to irreparable damage when it comes to familial bonds. When it comes to debt, blood is not always thicker than water!

All of these factors point to a crisis of disinvestment in American citizens' pursuit of higher education. But the crisis is not only about the loss of young people seeking higher education. It is equally about the emergence of the nefarious student lending industry, an industry that relies upon subsidies from the US government, taxpayer dollars, and squeezing money out of borrowers and co-signers with high interest rates for enormous profits. The dramatic rise of the student loan industry—the nuts and bolts, really, of "Higher Ed Inc."—was never part of the narrative to higher education for most Americans, but in fact, neither was college itself. So to understand how we got to where we are, we have to look briefly at the history of higher education in America to fully appreciate why this has become the fiasco it is.

The GI Bill: Access to higher education, upward mobility, and the expansion of the middle class

Prior to World War II in American history, most Americans did not even attend college. It was expensive and essentially reserved for the elite class of people in this country. The wealthiest went to Harvard, Yale, Stanford, Amherst, Princeton and others. There was even the tradition of having one's servants accompany students to school. Going even further back to the Colonial era, as the first institution of higher learning in the colonies, Harvard's first students had slaves accompany them.[9]

But a great opening up of higher education occurred in 1944, thanks to the GI Bill that funded millions of soldiers returning from the frontlines of the war. Whereas most schools were once only available to elites and their servants, nearly all soon became available to large swathes of the population. The GI Bill was unprecedented in how the federal government implemented public funding to millions of American citizens. With the GI Bill, college education was radically changed in the US, no longer the province of grooming just for the elite, but now integrated fully into middle-class life in America. Higher education suddenly became a right for a large majority of Americans, a meritocratic way to access upward mobility from working-class experiences that had previously been inescapable.

The GI Bill came about when it became clear that educating millions of soldiers, offering them jobs, and helping them buy homes were all important economic priorities that the government had a long-term interest in fostering. At that time, the country was still recovering from the Great Depression, when men and women went hungry and their children starved. Millions of people had been dispossessed from their homes, and one of the greatest American novels, *The Grapes of Wrath,* documented that dark, uncertain period of American history while condemning the inhumanity of the situation.

Policymakers had to reach a consensus about how to orchestrate all of these benefits for the millions of soldiers returning home, and they knew that the government was the best agent to take responsibility for creating policy and funding it. They were also fully aware of the fact that the poorest and least educated in Germany were the first to become attracted to the Nazi message. Roosevelt had already countered the Great Depression with the New Deal, but it was the war that pulled the country out of economic calamity, and now leaders knew they needed to offer returning soldiers a chance to start afresh after risking their lives on the battlefields across Europe to save democracy.

With President Franklin Delano Roosevelt still at the helm, lawmakers passed in 1944 the Servicemen's Readjustment Act, commonly referred to as the GI Bill. It authorized a range of benefits that made it affordable for returning soldiers to attend college, buy homes, and start small businesses. Although Roosevelt is generally given full credit for the bill, its first draft was actually drawn up by former Republican National Chairman Harry W. Colmery (yes, a Republican). The time Colmery spent in the military was a significant factor in his generosity of thought, and so the bill reflected his dedication to assisting veterans in readjusting to civilian life.

At one point Colmery warned Congress about the returning veterans, "They can make our country, or break it."

Like any form of major legislation, there was opposition. The President of Harvard at the time, James Conant, took an elitist position against it, insisting that the bill would allow for "the least qualified of the wartime generation" to attend colleges and universities. His staunchly anti-democratization view of higher education was not all that uncommon at the time. Fortunately, it fell on deaf ears, and the "Age of the GI Bill" began, as Edward Humes aptly called it. The US population would never be the same, particularly when it came to the opening up of higher learning and creating the perception that education was the key to individual prosperity for millions of people as well as a stepping stone to economic prosperity for the entire nation.

As a result of the GI Bill and subsequent government investment in higher education, the number of college students increased dramatically. Millions of young veterans who came from families with no college degrees were eager to be the first to graduate from colleges and universities across the US. Although black veterans did not benefit from the opportunity to take out mortgages like their white counterparts, the GI Bill did expand educational opportunities for them, too. In fact, it actually forced formerly all-white institutions of higher learning to open their doors to black veterans. Thus, many black veterans also went to college and beyond.

In the overall picture, before World War II, only 15% of Americans had the choice or opportunity to attend college. However, by 1947, 500,000 Americans graduated annually with a college degree, a figure more than three times higher than the approximately 160,000 who earned degrees in 1939. In 1947, 50% of students enrolled in Americans colleges were war veterans.

The GI Bill was unprecedented in how the federal government implemented public funding for higher education to millions of American citizens. Once the Servicemen's Readjustment Act was officially enacted, the Veterans Administration (VA) oversaw the distribution of the legislated aid to veterans.

The golden age of college education in America

The newly expanded accessibility to higher education and vocational training coincided with the most robust period of economic growth in the United States, and millions of Americans benefited from it. The 1950s and early 1960s are often referred to as the "Golden Age" of America, when between 8 and 9 million Americans found themselves part of a dynamic, innovative, and growing middle class.

Most social policy and economic experts agree that it is not coincidental that the rise of an enormous college-educated population led to the most significant economic boom in American history. The bill was clearly a major contributing factor to enabling America's Golden Age, a long, stable decade of growth that has never been collectively experienced since that time.

When the education and training part of the bill expired in 1956, a total of $14.5 billion had been disbursed to returning veterans. Although the government had taken a risk, that disbursement paid off. The Veterans Administration estimated the increase in federal income taxes alone paid for the cost of the bill several times over. By 1955, 4.3 million veterans had been granted home loans, with a total face value of $33 billion. This generation, referred to as the "greatest genera-tion," reaped huge benefits from the GI Bill, and allowed most of you reading this book to have the lives you probably grew up with. In the 1950s, the lingering fears of another depres-sion were quickly quelled and replaced with tremendous eco-nomic optimism and real growth.

The return on investing in the American people, overall, turned out to benefit the country in ways not seen since the passage of that bill. Out of all the world powers that fought in World War II, the US made the most enormous gains. Unlike European countries, the United States' infrastructure had not been devastated by the war, so that was already an advantage we had over European nations. But the GI Bill offered noth-ing but gains for the nation and a sense of being able to look forward to progress.

In contrast, the Baby Boomer generation, born between 1945 and 1964, and the subsequent generations, especially those who began attending college in the 1980s and onward, have had to fend for themselves for the most part. The federal government did not take risks on them, and they were not offered the opportunities that the greatest generation were pro-vided. There is a reason why WWII veterans always felt a sense of duty to their country after they returned from war: their country *invested* in them. Their country gave back to them.

One veteran said, "Thank God the government had the doors open for us,"[10] while another said about pursuing higher education, "It was a hell of a gift, an opportunity, and I never thought of it any other way . . . Sometimes I wonder if I really earned what I've gotten, to be frank with you."[11] Veterans like these would end up contributing enormously to their commu-nities, and they were provided the tools to do so as a result of the GI Bill and the national government's investment in higher education.

This is the opposite of the current situation for the majority of Americans who now attend college or university. Indeed, the majority of students today must go deeply into debt, especially those who come from economically disadvantaged homes, in order to attend school just to get a decent paying job. The story of the GI Bill versus the situation today provides us with a sharp contrast in how different the outcomes can be when the government chooses to invest rather than disinvest in its people.

This greatest generation was motivated at the personal level to be engaged not just with their immediate family, but with their communities as well as government at the local and federal levels. The GI Bill allowed wide access to education to different groups of people in the United States, especially when it came to higher education. In a word, higher education was no longer limited to white elites. With these gains, so many advantages after the war, and a newfound international influence, higher education in particular remained a chief interest at the federal level and in national politics. There was, however, a new (perceived) threat: The USSR and communism. Thus, investing in higher education would quickly become a matter of national security interest.

Perceived Cold War tensions: The National Defense Act (NDEA) and the USSR's Sputnik program

In 1958, fear suddenly struck the heart of the US when the Soviets successfully launched the Sputnik satellite into space, signaling that the Russians were ahead of the US in technology and space exploration, an implication that America's military superiority might be at risk. In response President Dwight D. Eisenhower signed the National Defense Education Act (NDEA) into law in an effort to counter the USSR's Sputnik Program. The Act was overseen through the Office of Education which at that time was part of the Department of Health, Education, and Welfare (HEW, a cabinet-level department that functioned from 1953 to 1979). [12]

Eisenhower described it as "short-term emergency legislation" to address the so-called 'Sputnik crisis.'[13] And it worked to some extent. Despite tensions and the threat of nuclear war between the two superpowers, Americans benefited from the Cold War when it came to educational opportunities that the NDEA made available. It was another case of how the federal government chose to invest in Americans and offer them funds for higher education as a way to bolster national security and combat ideologies—specifically communism à la the USSR—that was perceived as a threat to the American way of life.

In 1960, Arthur S. Flemming wrote "The Philosophy and Objectives of the National Education Act," a report which offers us a great deal of insight into the architecture behind NDEA and how Sputnik was perceived by top policymakers and military strategists in Washington, DC. When he wrote this essay, Flemming was a member of President Eisenhower's Advisory Committee on Government Organization, and prior to that, he had been appointed as Assistant to the Director of Defense Mobilization and eventually became Director of that Office. He was certainly a man who knew why this legislation was passed.

In the Abstract to the document, he wrote, "The National Defense Education Act recognizes that education is a unifying force, and it regards an educated citizenry as the country's most precious resource."[14] Flemming asserted the Act was intended to "motivate the discovery of intelligent and talented young men and women and stimulate them to devote themselves to the sciences, foreign languages, technology, and in general those intellectual pursuits that will enrich personal life, strengthen resistance to totalitarianism, and enhance the quality of American leadership on the international scene."[15]

What's clear about Flemming's view is that it reflects long-term thinking that investing in Americans is crucial to protecting the national security interests of the United States. It suggests that there are two benefits. First, higher education strengthens the interior world of the individual, creating a well-rounded, highly intelligent person. Second, it serves to fortify the idea that wherever Americans are or wherever they travel, they are representatives of US democracy, capable of not only defending the ideals of our American political system but leading others through the ideological principles instilled in them. With the perceived threat of the USSR, each educated person was thus deemed the "country's most precious resource."

Under NDEA and its funds, there was a special focus on high performing students who wished to pursue degrees in engineering, mathematics, modern foreign languages, as well as teaching. Title II of the NDEA saw the creation of the National Defense Student Loan (NDSL) Program, which offered low-interest federal loans to students. NDSL "provided study and military deferments and offered loan forgiveness of up to 50 percent at a rate of 10 percent per year for students who chose to serve as full-time teachers in public elementary or secondary schools." NDSL's name eventually was changed to the Perkins Loan after Congressman Carl Dewey Perkins (D-KY), who became a champion of the program. As of 2015 the program was being phased out.

The Higher Education Act of 1965

Over the next decades, the US government continued to invest in higher education. Several politicians saw opportunities to act in bold ways, and did just that. A significant piece of legislation occurred under the Johnson administration. On November 8th, 1965, on the campus of Southwest Texas State College (today Texas State University of San Marcos) far from the stuffy environs of Washington, DC, President Lyndon B. Johnson signed the Higher Education Act (the HEA).

Speaking to a crowd of faculty members, students, and parents on that day, Johnson said, "In a very few moments, I will put my signature on the Higher Education Act of 1965. The President's signature upon this legislation passed by this Congress will open a new door for the young people of America. For them, and for this entire land of ours, it is the most important door that will ever open—the door to education."

Johnson viewed education as part of his bigger agenda, the Great Society, whose two main goals were to eliminate institutionalized racial inequities and to eradicate poverty. Access to education was critical in overcoming those societal issues, and Johnson believed that a more educated populace meant a more robust democracy. The passage of this bill had been a hard battle for him, and there were plenty of skeptics. However, Johnson was not the least bit fazed by his opponents as he was a skilled politician who knew how to get his way.

Under Title IV of the HEA, financial aid provisions accomplished numerous goals, and additional provisions were added over the coming years and decades. For the purposes of this discussion, here are three significant provisions that were initially covered:

- It increased federal funding to universities;
- It created scholarships;
- It introduced low-interest rate loans to borrowers.

With the passage of HEA, millions of more young students were again able to pursue a college degree, something many of their parents never thought remotely possible. HEA launched college work-study programs, it authorized a summer school program for low-income students, and it launched Upward Bound (a program to help high school students attend college), and VISTA (Volunteers in Service to America, a Peace-Corps style program operating within the US and still in existence). It is worth noting that at the end of the day, Johnson managed to get bi-partisan support for HEA in Congress, something that is hard to comprehend today in light of contemporary political gridlock.

Shortly after HEA was signed, the Educational Opportunity Grant Program, a precursor to the famous Pell Grant program, was passed. With the passage of HEA, Johnson's involvement in education would set the stage for Jimmy Carter's own eventual establishment of the Department of Education.

The Carter administration and the creation of the Department of Education

Creating a specific separate Department of Education at the federal level was no easy task, despite the fact that it was a widely discussed for nearly a century. In the 1970s, it had been simply a division under Health, Education, and Welfare (HEW). The barrier to making education its own department was that federal involvement with education was enormously controversial. States feared losing control of education at the

local and state level. Many states resented the federal government getting involved in dictating how they should run their
educational systems and did everything they could to block
the establishment of a top level federal agency.

Despite these obstacles, President Jimmy Carter was
determined to change how education was approached by
Washington. In his memoir, Carter explained why he wanted
to create a separate department for education: "When I became
President, in spite of the importance of the subject, education
was still sometimes treated in Washington as an afterthought
or nuisance . . . Education programs were scattered all over
the federal bureaucracy, and there was no way for a coherent
policy to be considered or implemented." He continued, "During the 1976 campaign I had endorsed the idea of creating a
cabinet-level Department . . . Opposed by a variety of people
who saw advantages in the existing situation, including HEW
secretary Joe Califano, the formation of this department was
delayed until October 1979."[16] Califano, clearly defending his
turf at HEW, was not the only challenger though. Opposition
came from a multitude of other individuals as well as groups.

In the end Carter's efforts to not only successfully reorga-
nize the bureaucracy at the federal level and to actually establish a new department speaks volumes about his leadership
abilities. Carter and his administration were fully aware of
the history and tradition behind the objections to an education
department. But he understood education as a key element of
the public good, much like Johnson, and he believed the federal government ought to play a role in its direction.

When he signed S. 210 into law on October 19, 1979, Carter
said: "Education is our most important national investment. It
commands the time and attention of 60 million Americans—

3 citizens in 10. It consumes an annual public and private expenditure in excess of $120 billion. Every citizen has a vital, personal stake in this investment. Our ability to advance both economically and technologically, our country's entire intellectual and cultural life depend on the success of our great educational enterprise."[17]

Like Johnson, Carter believed the federal government had to play a positive role in Americans' lives, and hence why he created a cabinet level department. The Department of Education would serve a unifying purpose, as he explained:

> The time has passed when the federal government can afford to give second-level, part-time attention to its responsibilities in American education. If our Nation is to meet the great challenges of the 1980s, we need a full-time commitment at every level of government—federal, state, and local. The Department of Education bill will allow the federal government to meet its responsibilities in education more effectively, more efficiently, and more responsively.

Carter envisioned the Department of Education serving and supporting states, students, and higher education institutions.

At the same time the Department was created, Carter's political career was in jeopardy. Carter's flailing presidency and political troubles were related to a stagnant economy, which became a serious political problem for him. Hindsight's gift of perfect vision allows us to know that Carter was fighting a losing battle. For better or for worse, the health of the economy plays a tremendous role in presidential elections. Global markets were experiencing "stagflation," which in economic terms means that inflation is high and the economic growth rate is low. Americans found themselves struggling. Despite the complex reasons for why an economy surges, stagnates, or crashes, American voters tend to point fingers at the president. Carter became the fall guy and a one-term president.

As it would turn out, the Department of Education's bureaucratic evolution through today would not reflect the principles of the President who had established its existence. Since Carter did not serve a second term, it is hard to know what would have become of the Department if he had been in the White House for four more years.

Instead, Ronald Reagan's campaign platform in 1980 was dedicated to abolishing the newly formed cabinet level department, something that had a reverberating effect upon its bureaucratic functioning during his eight years as president. Reagan's policies set off what ultimately became our student debt financial crisis, a story we will begin examining next.

Chapter 3
Neoliberalism and Its Relationship to the Student Loan Debt Crisis

THERE ARE MOMENTS THAT DEFINE A PARADIGMATIC shift in the political and economic landscape of a country. In the case of Carter departing the White House, not only did his replacement mark a dramatic change in domestic policies in Congress, but also worldwide. It marked the beginning of the movement which came to be known as "neoliberalism."

This term is often misunderstood, in part, because the components of the word—*neo*, which means new, has positive connotations, and the word *liberal*, usually means open to new ideas and free. However, neoliberalism is essentially a reactionary movement, in that it is strongly anti-government and anti-regulation. It endorses a "laissez faire" type of capitalism, in which the government should step back and let capitalism function in whatever ways it does, because the market will weed out whatever elements of capitalism will not work. Or in the very least, government is only there to enforce "rules" of the market that benefit those who have consolidated control over capital.

As historian David Harvey explains in *A Brief History of Neoliberalism*, the movement altered public policy in government in profound ways never experienced prior to that time in American history. The institutionalization of neoliberalism was on the ascendancy in 1979, the same year the Department of Education was created, and Harvey asserts that the "consolidation of neoliberalism as a new economic orthodoxy" occurred just as two key figures, Margaret Thatcher and Ronald Reagan, took the reins of the government in their respective countries. Thatcher became Prime Minister of England in May of 1979, and shortly thereafter, in January of 1981, Ronald Reagan became president of the United States.

Both of these leaders played roles in dismantling the role of government in nearly every sphere of influence it formerly had. Reagan's presidency focused on deregulating markets as much as possible, claiming that government regulation was excessive and unnecessary in a market-driven capitalist economy.[18] In his view, markets needed to operate on their own and without the interference of the state. Reagan also went after welfare assistance to the poor that had been formulated under Johnson as a key element in his vision of The Great Society, claiming that those who were "dependent" upon so-called government hand-outs needed to be weaned from this troubling relationship and stand on their own. That brand of liberalism was perceived as the cause of all problems when understood through the lens of a neoliberal philosophical framework. The term "welfare state," especially when viewed by historians, social scientists, and economists, had not previously been seen in such a pejorative sense. However, once Reagan took office, a negative association became widespread.

Why was neoliberalism so erroneously appealing?

Defenders of neoliberalism insist that it benefits countries, local communities, and—most importantly—individuals. The founders of the movement and all its supporters, and the manufacturers of neoliberal economic policies believe it is the perfect melding of freedom with the capitalist market system. Thus, neoliberals both encourage and institute aggressive deregulatory policies. In their view, less government intervention—meaning less government oversight and regulatory enforcement—allows individuals and companies to pursue new markets. The pursuit of new markets and the accumulation of as much capital as possible are seen as two of the purest expressions of freedom.

The critics of neoliberalism, however, have another view, backed up by extensive academic research and evidence. This is a body of work that crosses multiple disciplines, all of which concludes that neoliberal policies are destructive, especially to poor and working-class people. David Harvey, Henry A. Giroux, Michael Thompson, and Naomi Klein, to name a few leading experts, have exhaustively outlined the history of the theory's development as well as the reasons why neoliberalism is based on erroneous logic and unproven economic concepts. Unfortunately, neoliberal economic policies have deeply affected people, political institutions, culture, education, and the environment, continuing on through today.

The concepts of little government intervention and regulation of the economy, the trickle-down theory of prosperity, and the anti-welfare stance and turn-a-blind-eye to income inequality attitudes of neoliberalism have led to the massive inequality that we now face today, whereby only 1% of the population has experienced an increase in wealth since the Reagan years of the 1980s. The neoliberal agenda has also done tremendous damage to both individual and collective freedom, as evidenced by its organized, political action against the poor, its assault on consumer rights, and its undermining of peoples' ability to be democratically engaged in voting.

Neoliberal economic policies have been especially disruptive of the US higher educational system. First, there has been a loss of influence of faculty members in administrative and bureaucratic matters relative to the governance of the university system overall. This is due to the increasing "corporatization" of universities, both public and private, in which administrative decisions are largely based on money.

Second, and related to that, is the fact that as the faculty are turned into part-time workforce, the administrative staff on the majority of campuses—both at public and private universities—has grown larger. Their salaries and benefits rival that of most faculty (even tenured professors), and they wield more power and influence as a result. This model is a top-down, hierarchical one, in which those at the top gain much, while those at the bottom—the students and part-time workers who teach them—continue to lose. (Chapter 5 details far more about the relationship between the universities and money.)

Third, as a result of the corporatization of universities, faculty members who enjoy tenure status are being replaced after their retirement by part-time instructors, although they have the same qualifications. While there are still tenure-track positions (lifetime positions once earned by the professor), these openings are disappearing at an alarming rate. The part-time faculty most often have no health care benefits, and certainly have little if any say about major decisions that the university makes, particularly when it relates to financial matters.

Finally, the neoliberal model influences cultural concepts of how groups, organizations, and individuals are defined. In the neoliberal world today, students are no longer really students whose intelligence is worth developing to help society, but instead are defined as consumers seeking out personalized education and training that will make them marketable and competitive once they join the workforce. This concept strips higher education of its previously respected relationship to the public good, a notion that has collective connotations, and relates to important concepts of civic duty and democratic engagement. This is the view of the role of education that nearly every president since Roosevelt has espoused, which I have detailed in this chapter.

More generally speaking, within a neoliberal system, the democratic rights of individuals and local communities are not only compromised, but severely threatened. While appearing to promote "free markets," neoliberalism is at its core really about the protection of private property for a small class of people, and the expansion of financial capital as the most crucial element of capitalism.

Neoliberalism varies when it comes to geographic location and implementation, but the general tenets are entirely recognizable. Overall, however, the United States is fast approaching an extreme version of neoliberalism in this new millennium wherein any sort of social safety net—remnants of a welfare state—have come close to being obliterated, thus making survival for the unemployed, many children, the ill, elderly, and the poor difficult and tenuous.

The privatization of everything under neoliberalism has transformed higher education such that it is now marketed as a commodity, and student loans are just another form of the "financialization" of debt. By contrast, in countries such as Germany, Sweden, Finland or Denmark, citizens are actually paid to go to college, whereas in the US, Americans must borrow heavily against their future earnings—if they are lucky enough to even find employment when they graduate—from the US government or private financial entities to pay for their education. Excessive borrowing to the tune of tens of thousands of dollars, which is now a necessity for most, is why we are facing a serious student loan debt crisis, and why we—as a nation—must face the facts about the predatory nature of the student lending industry and take a collective stand against "Higher Ed Inc."

The growing gap in accessibility:
Failing low-income students

As we reviewed, since the GI Bill, there have been many programs—some of which still exist—that were designed to help low-income students obtain grants to attend schools of higher education. There are, however, now several significant problems with such programs, especially the well-known Pell Loan Grant Program which was aimed at the nation's poor students who sought college educations.

First, these Pell grants often cover only a fraction of today's cost to attend college, especially at most four-year institutions, as the maximum amount for a Pell Grant for the academic year of 2015 through 2016 is $5,775. This is barely enough to cover the tuition fees at most colleges, yet alone living expenses. Furthermore, members of the GOP have especially been trying to drastically cut funding to the program for years, given their support for neoliberal policies over the facts.

This political fight to destroy Pell Grants began in 2012. The move wasn't especially new, but arguments from the GOP about social services being unnecessary had already been ramping up prior to this, particularly with the influence of the Tea Party and outsiders such as the Koch Brothers. While these groups have different ideologies, the target remains the same: the federal government. The idea for attacking the federal government's Pell Grants is founded on the same belief: a perception that anything—such as programs like Pell—run and operated by the federal government is bad, ineffective, and inefficient.

The fight over Pell began when a number of Tea Party Republicans put it on the chopping block, along with Medicare, Medicaid, and Social Security during the 2011 debt ceiling fiasco. In March of 2011, Representative Denny Rehberg (R-Montana), who at the time chaired the House Appropriations Subcommittee on Labor, Health and Human Services, Education, and Related Agencies, asserted that Pell was the same as welfare. Pell was saved, but only after subsidized loans for graduate students were slashed with the passage of the debt ceiling bill.

The political battle over Pell reemerged a year later in April of 2012, when the GOP attempted to severely cut the program's funding under a plan introduced by Congressman Paul Ryan (R-WI). Around that time, a panel discussion about Pell was held in DC with a host of experts speaking on the subject. Panelists were asked to answer the question: "Is the Pell Grant Program Sustainable?" One panelist, Dr. Jon Oberg, who had worked for the Department of Education, aptly replied:

I think it is the wrong question, not perhaps for the panel, but for the country [my emphasis]. I would be among those who believe that our federal investment in higher education, including investment in access and success for lower income students and our broader federal level of research at our institutions of higher education, should not be cut. If anything I would argue for increases . . . [we're] falling in international standing, and I'd like very much to talk about some comparatives, and look at other countries to see how they are able to do this, because we have a lot of lessons that I think we could learn.

Oberg was calling for additional investing in higher education with a thoughtful look at how other wealthy countries support and pay for higher education. José L. Cruz, the former Vice President of Higher Education Policy and Practice at The Education Trust, shared similar sentiments at the panel discussion:

I want to say that I am not only here as a representative of Education Trust, who works on these issues, and a member of the Save Pell Campaign, but also a former beneficiary of the Pell Grant Program.

Under fire, The Save Pell Campaign was launched in the Spring of 2012 by various think tanks and Democratic organizations. José Cruz responded to Ryan's plan to undermine the Pell Grant Program and sought to answer the question about Pell's sustainability, stating:

Are Pell Grants sustainable? The first things that comes to mind is that it is a flawed question . . . it's really not if we're willing or capable of sustaining the program, particularly . . . when it comes to opportunity deficits that we need to keep in mind. In quality, it is at an all-time low in America, it's on par with Tunisia, Sri Lanka, and Morocco. Social mobility is at an all-time low in America on par with Nepal and Pakistan . . . We all know that student loan debt in the US has reached the $1 trillion mark, surpassing credit card debt . . . So, if we feel there is worth in defending the democratic ideals of opportunity and social mobility, I think we cannot afford to say that we can't sustain the Pell Grant Program.

Cruz's answer points to the fundamental divide between the rather traditional liberal position that has existed for decades versus the neoliberal position reflected in Congressman Paul Ryan's bill. For Cruz and those members of Congress who believe in Pell, educating America's poorest students serves a valuable cause in terms of our democratic ideals of egalitarianism—providing economic opportunity and upward mobility to the poor. In the eyes of neoliberals, however, keeping the government and taxpayer money out of education, and not believing there is any reason to give poor students grants for college is motivation enough to defund Pell.

As August 2013 neared, the debt ceiling once again became a huge political and economic battle between Democrats and Republicans. While no other president has ever been refused the raising of the debt ceiling, Congress, specifically Tea Party reactionaries, have battled President Barack Obama over and over again on it, contributing to overwhelming levels of dysfunction in government that we have had to endure for nearly a decade. In effect, the Pell Grant program has become a casualty of the debt ceiling debate, as an army of neoliberal politicians constantly push for austerity measures. There is no doubt that the program will certainly be threatened again.

There is, however, a darker side to the Pell Grant program that needs to be revealed, a fraud being committed that is shocking and should provoke us to rise up against this travesty. This is the fact that Pell Grants are now being used to benefit economically advantaged students at the expense of needier students. Yes, that's right! Studies have found that Pell Grants aren't even going to those students who need them the most. The explanation behind this is complicated, but it's worth unpacking this issue, as everyone must begin to see the light for what is happening behind the curtains here.

Inverting Pell's original purpose and college's race to the top

As higher education policy analyst Steve Burd argues, Pell is being 'undermined' by the universities in an elaborate 'shell' game. (I would add that there is another party at fault here, too, what I call the enrollment management cartels, which I will discuss in greater detail in Chapter 5.) This practice, as Burd shows, has been common at private universities, but now public universities are adopting similar tactics based on what is called "net price"—meaning the amount students pay after all grant aid has been exhausted. This hurts low-income students. Burd says, "As more states cut funding for their higher education systems, public colleges are increasingly adopting the enrollment management tactics of their private college counterparts—to the detriment of low-income and working-class students alike."

The way the game works, according to Burd, is that colleges offer poor students only a small amount of a Pell Grant, far from the amount they might deserve. In most cases, the students must decline the offer, as they do not have the resources to supplement the Pell Grant with enough of their own money to afford the college. As a result, the college ends up with extra funds from declined Pell Grants that they can offer wealthier students, in an effort to attract higher-income families who are more valuable in the long-term to the college.

Burd's study found that schools like Penn State University did not offer their poor students any sort of break in relation to other students. Furthermore, at the flagship campus, students pay $16,000 a year, which is more than double that of most four-year colleges and universities of similar status. Hundreds of schools like the Penn State University system, as Burd points out, are not just looking for the best and brightest, but also the wealthiest, thus creating economic inequality on campuses across the US.

This is a significant reason why, even after increases in Pell Grant funding, the college-going gap between low-income students and their wealthier counterparts remains as wide as ever today. Low-income students simply do not receive the full benefits intended for them. This shell game issue raises even more disturbing questions. Indeed, one wonders: how are all of funds being allocated by the universities and colleges? Furthermore, how are they are being used since there is little, if any, oversight?

The dark future of Neoliberalism

The juxtaposition between higher education and neoliberalism is subtle in the United States, so I hope this brief explanation has raised questions in your mind about the impact it has had on American citizens, especially students. Neoliberalism's policies have had a tremendous influence on creating the student lending industry itself, i.e., how it operates in terms of a system that profits from the "financialization" of debt, and how education overall—not just higher education—is perceived by those who are shaping and implementing policy directives.

The fact that neoliberalism took time to fully ingrain itself into government and has appeared in pockets across the globe is testament to the long process it takes to establish a new economic theory and supporting structures and policies. Since it strips large groups of people and communities of their former freedoms and privileges, it has been met with stark resistance, which in turn has caused many instances of state sanctioned violence against protestors. One only has to look at what occurred when Occupy Wall Street flourished and spread across the US to see the violent tactics that peaceful protesters encountered in those cases. Police crackdowns on these groups, as well as on journalists reporting live from the protests, were swift and often harsh, using pepper-spray, mass arrests, and other types of questionable actions that groups such as the American Civil Liberties Union (ACLU) criticized and condemned at the time.

It needs to be emphasized that neoliberalism did not come crashing out of the sky overnight, just as the evisceration of higher education as a public good did not either. Both took place over the course of several decades. Like a frog put in bowl of cold water which is then slowly heated without the frog noticing, people do not observe how severe and drastic neoliberal changes in policy become when they are introduced slowly. It becomes increasingly a "normal" practice that higher education transforms from a public good to a costly job training program and a commodity that only the wealthy can afford. The architects of neoliberal policies who crudely and cruelly used Latin American countries in the 1970s and 1980s as live laboratories (think of so many South American banana republics!) perhaps learned a lesson about using a slower implementation of their philosophy when it came to the United States. As for its chief architects, it was a group of economists at the University of Chicago, Milton Friedman being the most well-known of them, who championed neo-liberal thinking and sought to implement it into the core of American political thinking.[19] Friedman's economic model is diametrically opposed to the Keynesian model of economics, which, in order to fully understand neoliberalism, must be defined and contrasted so you can recognize the underpinnings of this argument against neoliberalism.

Keynesian economics was implemented during the Great Depression in the US by British economist John Keynes (1883–1946). Keynes believed in an interventionist state, that is, he endorsed the idea that government should play a significant role in social justice in economics. This means the state should be involved with solving issues related to unemployment, health care, and education. The Keynesian model was fully adopted by European countries and the US in the 1950s and 1960s. It was during this time, as mentioned earlier regarding the period of the GI Bill, the United Stated enjoyed significant growth during those two decades. But that would soon come to an end.

The 1970s was a period of economic stagnation and market crises, which would only worsen during the 1980s. At this time, leaders began to question the Keynesian economic model, one that had been in place for decades. Of course, there were a number of complex reasons—the desire to consolidate power into the hands of a small global elite, to control unstable global markets, to fix geopolitical issues—that allowed political leaders like Thatcher and Reagan to justify their reasons for abandoning Keynesian economics. Furthermore, prior to Thatcher and Reagan assuming power, the 1970s was a period of high unemployment and inflation worldwide. These two factors led to numerous fiscal crises.

Thus, it appeared that Keynesian policies were no longer working, and a backlash ensued. The 1980s marked the beginning of an assault on the many so-called entitlement programs, including government support of investment in higher education. This launched the beginning of the student loan debt crisis, as the attacks on higher education were (and continue to be) carried out by powerful institutions and individuals who aggressively promote free market rhetoric and insist that governments remain staunchly non-interventionist, even when it comes to serving the public good. Privatization of services that were once operated by the "welfare state"—education, health care, social programs, and even prisons—became the goal of neoliberals.

Today, proponents of neoliberal policies, those who espouse free market economics and various euphemisms for trickle-down economics, fill think tanks all over Washington, DC. Their neoliberal rhetoric serves to pollute public discourse, intentionally distorting the public's understanding of serious issues, especially the one related to higher education as a public good. PR spin aside, there is a something very concrete occurring here, something real that all Americans must pay attention to—in the US, we are presently witnessing the most aggressive form of welfare dismantlement to ever occur. This is truly a historic moment, but one with potentially dangerous results for the majority of Americans, especially when it comes to the future collective intelligence of our country. If the majority of our youth do not attend college, we will become a nation of "stupids" who cannot compete with the rising nations of the planet. The neoliberals protecting their own wealth will slowly persuade us that their policies make sense, and like that frog, we will all slowly cook ourselves into oblivion.

Higher education, in and of itself, produces an informed, intelligent citizenry, and should always be respected as an investment in America. We must abandon the notion that higher education should be limited to the best and the brightest people as long as they have the money to pay for their diplomas. We must move away from this idea that unless a degree is valued according to "the market," then it is frivolous. Even President Barack Obama recently made a disparaging remark about a student studying art history that was uncalled for. Again, the value of a degree lies in becoming a critically engaged citizen, capable of contributing to the public good, participating intelligently in the important discourse of society to create, innovate, and improve our nation and the entire planet. In order to meet the challenges that we are facing as a species, one of the biggest ones being climate change, we need to invest in people and that means investing in higher education. We need to pique young people's curiosity at institutions of higher learning and support them on multiple levels, including financial support. In so doing, these students can leave their universities with diplomas in hand and be filled with ideas about how to improve things in the world, instead of leaving with a pile of debt and a mind occupied with fears of how to cover rent and the basic cost of living each month.

Given this background, it is critical that we recognize that neoliberal politicians, if not voted out of office soon, will literally alter the fabric of America.

Chapter 4

Student Loans: Total Complexity, Total Lack of Transparency

SINCE THERE ARE SO MANY TYPES OF STUDENT LOANS, this creates a lot of confusion for borrowers. This chapter intends to dispel that confusion in order to clarify the options that have been available to borrowers, parents of borrowers, and co-signers. In doing this, this chapter is also intended to point out why the student loan industry is failing us and needs to be radically restructured.

A cloudy soup of loans

The mechanics behind student loans are not only complex, but deliberately misleading, something I believe was, if not intentionally created, has certainly been perpetuated by some of the architects behind "Higher Ed Inc." The level of misinformation begins as soon as a student starts the process of taking out a loan and it often does not end until the lifetime of the loan is over.

Many Americans do not even know that the source of their student loans is predominantly the federal government, which then has contracts with private enterprises to service them. In a survey taken several years ago, 50% of those surveyed believed that student loans were funded from private sources, not the government.

There is a good reason for their confusion, since four of the largest lenders[20]—Nelnet (NNI), Navient,[21] Great Lakes, and the Pennsylvania Higher Education Assistance Agency (PHEAA)—are all private organizations that have servicing contracts with the Department of Education. They thus appear to be "private" but they are not. This misunderstanding leads to a great deal of confusion among consumers and taxpayers, particularly when one considers that taxpayers are funding a large industry that is designed to keep a large majority of Americans who attend institutions of higher learning in debt, while the industry players earn gobs of profits. Seems strange to me that taxpayers want their money to go to making an elite group of lenders richer by the day.

The public is not just unaware about where loans originate, they also lack knowledge about the funding and payoff process itself, and how the industry effectively preys on the inexperience of borrowers. Consider the average age of most borrowers—18 and fresh out of high school—and the financial decision that they must make, one that will affect both their personal life and financial outcomes for the rest of their lives. When it comes to student loans, despite their complex nature and how they lead so many into a lifetime of indentured servitude, this is the age when most college-bound people sign on the dotted line with very little understanding of how much money they will eventually owe and whether their future salaries might be able to afford it. The process of filling out the FASFA form is as perplexing to borrowers of any age as well as it is to their parents, regardless of their socioeconomic background.

Another point of misinformation is the fact that college financial aid offices put packages together for students and don't necessarily share all the information with them. Thus when it comes to choices of loan sources for borrowers, parents and students seldom realize that they might have been able to negotiate for better terms. There is a mistaken perception that a student must accept whatever is offered. On top of that, many families do not even understand the difference between a loan and a grant. A grant is free money from the government or from non-governmental entities, money that does not need to get paid back.

Some savvy students and their families can negotiate their loan, for example, telling the financial aid office, "I'd like more grants to offset the amount of loans I am taking out." Of course, those who have this type of leverage tend to be wealthy and have influence. In these cases, these families often benefit from the free money of grants, because the university where the student has been accepted is trying to attract upper middle-class or wealthy students for branding purposes. In so doing, it is often at the expense of assisting lower-income students.

Thus it is important to understand that financial aid offices are not in the business of transparency. While financial aid officers believe they are there to help students, they are in fact really money pushers for a predatory lending system. The less the borrower understands how things work, the less transparency the loan process has used. The more the schools, the lenders, and the enrollment management cartels control the money, the better it is for those who maintain the power. In the end, the student serves as a pawn for the eventual extraction of capital for years, decades, sometimes even a lifetime for the profits of the lenders.

Since 94% of students take out student loans,[22] understanding the mechanics raises an important question: Why is the loan process so difficult for borrowers to understand? In my view, the answers show that is intentional or at least no thought has been given to be honest and fair with student borrowers.

First, the paperwork is daunting. For instance, for every semester a student enrolls in classes and takes out loans, a *new* loan is issued. As absurd as it sounds, it makes no business sense that a student can end up with as many as eight different loans over the course of a four-year college degree, one for each semester.

The actual disbursement of money is odd, too. The aid goes directly from the lender into the schools' financial aid office, rather than to the student. This point is important because before the money is ever available to the student, it goes through institutional hands before reaching her pocket.

This process ultimately leaves the borrower with little understanding of how and where she is receiving her funds. Indeed, she fills out a FAFSA form with little information on how the form gets translated into a decision about her financial aid, unless she does exhaustive research on what that document means at the Department of Education's site and by experts on the subject. Once she is finished with the FAFSA form, the institutions—the lenders and the financial aid offices—make the determination about what sorts of loans and grant money will be allocated to her, and finally, the financial aid office receives the money.

Breaking down the types of loans

For these reasons, it is crucial to dissect each type of loan and be sure you understand them. Overall, there are four categories of loans:

- Stafford and Perkins Student Loans
- Parent Loans (also known as PLUS loans)
- Private Student Loans (Private-Private Loans)/ Alternative Student Loans
- Consolidated Loans

Stafford and Perkins Student Loans

Stafford loans used to be divided into two categories—The Federal Family Education Loan Program (FFEL or FFELP) and the Federal Direct Student Loan Program, otherwise known as Direct Loans (DL).

The first of these, the FFEL program, was launched in 1965 and while in operation, it lent close to $889 billion to students. Although the program is now defunct and no new FFEL loans have been originated after passage of the Health Care and Education Reconciliation Act on May 26, 2010, hundreds of billions of dollars of outstanding FFEL loans continue to be serviced and collected by lenders and servicing outfits. For example, Sallie Mae has over $118 billion in former FFEL loans that have yet to be repaid, which serves as a major cash flow and asset for the company.

As a result, only the second of these types, the DL Stafford Loans, remain available. DL loans can be either *subsidized*, which means that the government pays the interest while the student attends school, or *unsubsidized*, meaning the student pays the interest. The student may also defer payments on the loan, plus the interest until graduation. It should be noted that effective July 2012, subsidized Stafford loans were no longer available to graduate students.

Meanwhile, in contrast to Stafford Loans, Perkins loans are granted to students who can demonstrate great financial need. The interest rates are usually only about 5%, lower than DL loans. However, the Perkins program was at risk of being shut down at the time of this writing.

What does repayment look like for these federal loans? Essentially, repayment schedules are within the range of 10 to 25 years long. The borrower's university is supposed to inform the individual of repayment options upon enrollment and again at graduation. There are also "exit counseling sessions." But in some cases, these meetings never take place, thus leaving borrowers and their parents totally in the dark about their repayment schedule and other details.

Parent Loans (also known as PLUS Loans)

If a student cannot qualify for enough financial aid to cover the cost of tuition, books, room, and board, parents can opt to take out additional loans, called Parent PLUS loans. These loans actually originate from the same Direct Loan Program as student loans come from, but they are given out to parents. (Until 2010, there had been FFEL PLUS loans, too).

There is no cumulative limit on these types of loans, meaning that parents can borrow significant sums of money on behalf of their children. Many parents misunderstand PLUS loans and presume that these are another type of private loan.

Unfortunately, those who have taken out Parent PLUS loans and are suffering the consequences have not been well documented. This group of borrowers remains sorely unaccounted for, something that will most likely change as the crisis continues to worsen. As Tamar Lewin, a New York Times reporter who has been covering higher education for several decades wrote in a 2013 article, "Child's Education, but Parents' Crushing Loans:"

There are record numbers of student borrowers in financial distress, according to federal data. But millions of parents who have taken out loans to pay for their children's college education make up a less visible generation in debt. For the most part, these parents did well enough through midlife to take on sizable loans, but some have since fallen on tough times because of the recession, health problems, or lives that took a sudden hard turn.

And unlike the angry students who have recently taken to the streets to protest their indebtedness [Occupy Wall Street], most of these parents are too ashamed to draw attention to themselves. [...]

In the first three months of this year [2013], the number of borrowers of student loans age 60 and older was 2.2 million, a figure that has tripled since 2005. That makes them the fastest-growing age group for college debt. All told, those borrowers owed $43 billion, up from $8 billion seven years ago, according to the Federal Reserve Bank of New York.

This group of parents serves as yet another example of how predatory and broken the student lending industry is at a *systemic level* when considering the scale of the problem. I have collected many anecdotal tales from parents who have taken out loans or who are co-signers on their child's loans and their stories are as heart-wrenching as the students. But what is most important to consider from a policy perspective is the broader implications these figures are having on the health of local economies and the national economy, given how many parents are significantly impoverished by needing to pay off their children's college loans.

Private Student Loans (Private-Private Loans)/
Alternative Student Loans

Since the lines are blurred when differentiating between so-called federal loans and private loans, i.e., because the majority of federal loans are serviced and handled by private lenders, as indicated at the beginning of the chapter, I will therefore refer to these loans as "private-private student loans" because the money does indeed come from private sources and is doled out by private companies.

Private-private student loans are an alternative form of loans from private banks such as Wells Fargo or credit unions. The government is not involved in funding these loans and they are purely a loan instrument that these institutions offer and on which they intend to make a profit, just like a home, car, or boat loan.

While there had been a spike in loans from private banks prior to the financial crisis in 2008, some banks have pulled out of the private-private student loan business entirely, such as Bank of America and Chase Bank. Nevertheless, there still is business in the private-private student lending industry.

Even Sallie Mae, the private institution that sets up federal government loans has gotten into the action. When it split into two separate entities (renaming part of the company as

Navient), the private-private loan realm became the focus of one of its branches. As the *Wall Street Journal (WSJ)* reported, the decision was made in part "in a bid at boosting market valuation." At the same time, the former Chief Operating Officer John F. Remondi of Sallie Mae became the CEO of the education-management side of the company, replacing the now infamous Albert L. Lord. When the announcement was made, Remondi made it clear to investors that Sallie Mae was doing just fine despite FFEL being brought to an end. He was quoted in the *WSJ* as saying that for a long period of time, "we were very frustrated with the valuation of the company . . . [but] what's different now is clearly the significantly improved financial position of the company."

Why did Remondi say that the company was now doing better? It's because one side of the company, the education-management side, purchased the old FFEL loans from smaller loan holders, in essence gobbling up still profitable FFEL loan repayments that other institutions wanted to be rid of. Meanwhile, the business side that doles out private-private loans was looking to expand into the consumer debt market. This type of diversification turns people into debtors in a multitude of ways and serves to generate high revenues for the company. Their business model is not very different than the payday loan industry which generates large amounts of high interest payments and fees from millions and millions of Americans, many of whom are the most economically vulnerable in this country.

When it comes to understanding private-private loans as debt traps, it is also important for borrowers to understand the risks that come with taking out these sorts of loans.[23]

Here are key things to keep in mind when considering private-private loans:

- They are not subsidized by the federal government. As such, interest accrues as soon as the loan is obtained from Day 1.

- These are also the riskiest loans to take on as a borrower, because interest rates can vary dramatically and are generally much higher than loans from the federal government.

- Grace periods for deferring these loans once borrowers leave school, either upon graduating or by dropping out, are generally only offered once, and usually last only 6 months to a year.

It is ultimately inadvisable to take out private-private student loans because the leverage a borrower has is limited. However, even private banks and credit unions have come to realize that the volume of non-payments of student loans has hurt their portfolios, so they have started to be slightly more open to negotiating with struggling borrowers to at least be paid back partially.

But private lenders have tremendous power, especially when it comes to repayment schedules. Not surprisingly, they have ensured that legislation be written in their favor. For example, nearly all private-private loans require a co-signer, and it becomes the co-signer's 100% responsibility to pay back the loans on time if the borrower becomes delinquent. This is another part of the permanent trap of indebtedness, as it often causes terrible problems in relationships as co-signers may turn on borrowers who were formerly family members or loved ones. Co-signing is effectively a recipe for disaster when it comes to maintaining healthy relationships among family members and friends. This is a burden for both borrower and the co-signer, reminding us again of the human cost of the student loan debt debacle.

One borrower wrote to me several years ago and told me about his relationship with his co-signer who was his grand-mother. The relationship had not only soured, but had come to an end—with his own grandmother!

It is also a commonly known fact that financial problems are the number one reason for the dissolution of marriage. Compound that with a large private-private loan debt (I am also speaking from my own personal experience) and—even the strongest couples with the best bonds, the union can quickly fall apart as a result of this type of burden.

Consolidated Loans

Consolidated loans are simply lumping lots of loans together in a new package and repayment schedule. Supposedly done to simplify repayment schedules, they can be an even worse burden. Once locked into an agreement to consolidate loans, the borrower can't change her mind and "unconsolidate" in order to reconsolidate with another lender who might offer a cheaper loan rate.

This lock-down is unheard of elsewhere in the loan indus-try. If this were the case with home mortgages, then a home buyer would *never* be able to refinance and would be stuck with the original lender from whom they took out the loan(s) to mortgage a home. In all likelihood, it would be protested wildly everywhere in America. Even car loans are able to be refinanced if a lower rate becomes available.

Another common problem with consolidated loans is that the borrower will often pay more over the lifetime of the loan after consolidation. In addition, they may lose their borrowing rights on other types of loans. This is especially true if they consolidate formerly federal student loans into a private-private consolidation loan, making it difficult for them to borrow on other loans.

With these drawbacks to loan consolidation, what are the benefits? For starters, consolidation allows borrowers to make one monthly payment. It may also enable them to pay lower payments. That is why borrowers must carefully weigh the pros and cons before deciding whether or not to consolidate their loans.

Several congressional offices over the past few years have introduced legislation that would enable borrowers to refinance their student loans. Senator Sherrod Brown (D-OH) tried to introduce legislation to fix some of the problems, and more recently Senator Elizabeth Warren (D-MA) has led another effort to introduce new refinancing legislation. However, all efforts are always vehemently opposed by the GOP, so these well-intentioned bills are crushed without a chance of ever being enacted and bringing any sort of relief to debtors.

The subcategories of loans make it even worse

Now that the categories of each type of loan have been defined, there are subcategories to these loans, another factor that causes confusion for borrowers. The following subcategories are:

Direct Subsidized Stafford Loans for undergrads

These loans are at a fixed interest rate, currently 4.3%. However, since July 2012 there has been a battle raging on the Hill about this rate expiring, as it would then double. When the debate began in 2012, the Presidential election was in full swing, and President Obama was urging Congress to keep the interest rates at 4.3%. If Congress failed to act—and there were Republicans who wanted to let the rate expire and then double—the rates would have jumped to 6.8% for 7.4 million borrowers who were in school. However, Republican Presidential candidate Mitt Romney came out in support of President Obama's stance, and so the rates did not double in 2012.

But the battle on rates for these loans was hardly won. It reemerged again in 2015, and Democrats, such as Senator Warren, have taken up the issue. Frustratingly, perhaps even for Democrats who focused on the interest rate issue, this problem fails to fully address the way in which millions of borrowers are struggling or unable to pay off their loans and thus continue to languish under crushing debt.

Unsubsidized Stafford Loans for undergraduates and graduate students (or individuals seeking professional degrees)

Unsubsidized Stafford Loans are fixed at 6.8%. These loans do not require that a borrower prove she has financial need for the loan. Borrowers have the choice of either paying the interest on these loans while in school or deferring the interest until after graduation. If the borrower chooses the latter option—not to pay interest while she is enrolled—then the interest accrues and is capitalized, i.e., the interest owed is added to the original principal of the amount borrowed. This means that the borrower has to pay interest on the interest not paid, thus making it even harder to pay off the loan after graduation.

Direct Unsubsidized Loans for undergrads and graduates

Like Unsubsidized Stafford Loans, these loans are at a fixed rate of 6.8%. However, these loans have "loan origination fees" which means borrowers pay points to get these loans, similar to paying points on a mortgage. The website studentaid.ed.gov states, "The origination fee is a percentage of the amount of each loan you receive. For loans first disbursed on or after July 1, 2010, the loan origination fee is 1.0%. We will deduct the loan origination fee proportionately from each loan disbursement. The specific loan origination fee that you are charged will be reflected in a disclosure statement that we send to you."

This means that the fee is deducted from the amount loaned before the borrower receives it. The borrower must pay back the total amount of the loan, including the loan origination fee.

Variations on Private-Private Loan interest rates

Interest rates on private-private loans are not always fixed and may vary—like a variable mortgage rate. Some can be reasonable, while others can be high. For instance, Chase Bank's "Select Private Loans," when they were still offered, varied with margins of interest between 3.33% and 9.23%.

An intentionally complex system

The description of the many varieties of loans and how they differ provides a clear picture as to why borrowers and their parents (or other potential co-signers) find the system to be befuddling, daunting, and lacking in transparency. Moreover, most borrowers and their families do not fully grasp how loans are broken down, i.e., what sorts of loans they are taking on, who or what entity disburses them, and how they are collected when repayment schedules commence.

In short, it comes down to truly understanding who gets what and why? The answer to that question is not as easy as it may appear, because it is not very straightforward, despite the plethora of pamphlets and websites dedicated to loan information.

There are numerous and complex reasons for why it is this way. First, financial aid offices are—unwittingly or not—lacking in transparency (and I'll explain this in chapter 5). Second, there has been a widening gap between college affordability for low-income students and minorities versus wealthier, privileged students, which has resulted in colleges shifting funding from needier students to those less in need.

That seems like an oxymoron. but a study published by the New America Foundation in May 2013 found that the commitment to breaking down the "financial barriers" to higher education for low-income and working-class Americans has been steadily eroding. While higher education used to be a means by which lower-income and working-class Americans could gain entry to the middle class and even beyond, the debt loads these particular students are acquiring set them back further.

Furthermore, the levels of indebtedness among poorer students are part of a strategy connected to the education management and enrollment industry, a private sector industry with which many Americans are not familiar. This industry reaps huge profits when hired by colleges and universities in order to attract the "best and the brightest." Studies have shown that low-income students for whom the management and enrollment companies could be competing do not even apply to top-tier colleges. They are not recruited very hard and they have an intuitive sense they will not receive enough money in grants or loans. The consequences to this unraveling of a previously meritocratic system, especially at non-profit state universities, is troubling, as will be discussed in Chapter 5: The Complicity of the Universities.

While the bulk of outstanding student debt is in the form of federal loans, private-private loans are becoming more of a necessity as tuition continues to rise at dramatic levels. Banks have loaned approximately $150 to $200 billion in private-private student loan debt (that is, the private-private student loans mentioned earlier or those not connected to the federal government in any way). That enormous figure, however, could potentially worsen with each passing year, due to deep and continued budget cuts to state funding for public universities, forcing tuitions up and students to borrow more.

In addition, private lenders also target low-income borrowers with high cost loans. After all, it is easier to make high profits off of millions of low-income people rather than just a few, and that is the model they are following. Obviously, low income students struggle to pay back their loans. This is especially true of those who do not graduate. Rates of default for this group of borrowers are the highest. The same is true of those who attend the burgeoning number of for-profits colleges. Many of these institutions have turned out to be bogus, failing to graduate a large majority of their students. Indeed, 50% of students who attend a for-profit college default on their loans.

In short, "Higher Ed Inc." has made it a business to turn Americans, particularly those who are the most vulnerable, into permanent debtors so that a small elite profit.

Delinquency and default

Default rates on student loans have been alarmingly high in recent years, all of which began shortly after the Great Recession in 2008. This should come as no surprise to many Americans, given how most households have seen their dollar stretched, while also experiencing job loss or hours cut in the workplace. Meanwhile, the cost of living has only continued to increase.

The statistics about defaulting raise important questions: First, what happens when a person is delinquent on her loans? Second, what are the consequences of defaulting on the loans?

The ramifications of delinquency and defaulting vary depending upon the type of loan affected. If someone becomes delinquent in paying back federal loans, they are eligible for deferment or forbearance. There are different forms to complete to become eligible for these types of delays in repayment— a type of pause for borrowers repaying their loans—and the Department of Education urges borrowers to reach out to the loan servicers to whom they are having trouble repaying their loans in a timely manner. Federal loans are eligible for the Income Based Repayment Program (IBR), Income Contingent Repayment (ICR), and PAYE (Pay As You Earn), though all of these have limitations and restrictions that make them a non-solution to the larger student debt debacle in the US.

Private-private loans are a different matter. In some cases, delinquency, meaning that the borrower is behind on a repayment schedule, is completely disallowed, as some lenders will declare a borrower immediately to be in default if even a single payment is late by just one month. When this occurs, the borrower is turned over to collections and not just sought, but hunted down ruthlessly. Private lenders are also overwhelmingly inflexible when working with distressed borrowers, allowing no leeway for paying late.

However, unlike federal loans, there is generally a statute of limitations for collections efforts for private loans. This means that, depending on the state, the lender cannot pursue debtors in the same manner in which the federal government is able to pursue them. While this may sound like a good thing for debtors, the fact is, it generally does not work out in his or her favor, as judges quite often rule in favor of the lender. This effectively means that private lenders can be just as aggressive as the government when pursuing collections from distressed borrowers.

Judges do, in some cases, rule in favor of debtors. A recent ruling in October of 2015, for example, deemed that student lending companies were not above the law.[24] The ruling took place in the Fourth Circuit Court of Appeals with a case in which the Pennsylvania Higher Education Assistance Agency (PHEAA) argued that it had the right to "sovereign immunity." If the Court of Appeals had ruled in PHEAA's favor, it would have resulted in barring consumers from pursuing legal action, specifically the right to sue. In that case, the court decided that consumers (debtors) could sue PHEAA. Despite this favorable outcome, such rulings, while encouraging, are few and far between when debtors come out ahead. Moreover, they do little to solve the deep problems of the student loan debt debacle or the enormous systemic problems that "Higher Ed Inc." has created and continues to perpetuate.

Defaulting on federal loans differs. First, if a borrower defaults on federal loans, collectors are assigned by the Department of Education to collect the money. These collectors are often subsidiaries of Navient (formerly Sallie Mae) and other lending companies, making it a clear conflict of interest. Collectors, not surprisingly, use aggressive tactics, because the Department of Education awards them bonuses based upon how much money they collect from the borrower. In 2012, for example, collection agencies received commissions of over $1 billion. In some cases, the Department of Education awards commissions as high as 20% on recovered loans.

Indeed, the overreach and power of collectors is staggering. Their collections people that work for the Department of

Education are ruthless when collecting on defaulted loans. Getting out of the debt through bankruptcy is impossible with federal loans. The same is true of those who operate private collections.

With the passage of the Bankruptcy Abuse Prevention and Consumer Protection Act in 2005, in fact, it has become virtually impossible to discharge private student loans through bankruptcy. Recently, borrowers who have become delinquent on loans have told me that lenders have threatened to put liens on their co-signers' homes. The feds are also now going after people in court and seizing property and liquid assets.

Ironically, the Obama administration ran on a platform for the 2012 election that claimed to help "average folks" get to college and obtain degrees. At the same time, under this administration's watch, the Congressional Budget Office (CBO) cited that the Obama administration projected in 2014 the government would make a $51 billion profit from student loan borrowers.

When defaulting on a loan, while private companies may reap the benefits, it is grave and ruinous for an individual. Once a borrower has defaulted, the federal government can garnish the person's wages, future or current Social Security benefits, disability checks, and deduct money from income tax refunds. Defaulting on student loans of any kind destroys a person's credit, and can also prevent an individual from having a professional license in certain fields of work.

Not only do the feds go after student borrowers and defaulters through collection agencies, they are now using a different place to exert their money collection muscle: the court room. For example, according to a 2012 article in the *Sun Sentinel* entitled "Feds cracked down on South Florida student loan defaulters," the feds are now filing lawsuits against student loan defaulters. The federal government has always had this ability to use the courts to take legal action against delinquent borrowers, but in the past they had not taken such action or did so infrequently as to not be newsworthy. The reporter of this story, however, noted, "the feds sued 4,328 people nationwide, a 43 percent increase since 2010." With high rates of unemployment as well as underemployment, along with it being essentially impossible to discharge student loan debt through bankruptcy, the state is coming down hard on those with little resources. This seizure of money through the court system illustrates again how the "financialization" of debt is taking a toll on communities and families across the nation.

A note on the so-called "Rehabilitation" programs

There are rehabilitation programs for debtors of defaulted loans, though suggestions have been made to improve this approach. For instance, on March 27, 2012, House and Senate Republican leaders submitted a letter to the General Accountability Office (GAO) expressing concern that the rehabilitation program, which helps borrowers restore their credit, was not functioning properly. In the letter they wrote:

> [W]e are increasingly concerned the department may not be appropriately managing student debt, particularly when helping borrowers who have defaulted on their loan payments.
>
> Under the Direct Loan program, borrowers who are in default can 'rehabilitate' their loan and return their credit to good standing by making a certain number of consecutive payment on their loans. Unfortunately, we recently heard

from a borrower who claims to have made the required amount of on-time payments in an effort to rehabilitate his loan, but, due to the department's delays, is unable to remove the black mark of default from his credit report and take advantage of better repayment options.

As part of our oversight responsibilities, it is important for us to understand challenges with the Direct Loan program. Bureaucratic problems within the department that are creating additional issues for borrowers could have serious implications not only for the Direct Loan program, but also for the financial stability of all student loan borrowers.

These concerns are legitimate about how loans are rehabilitated. However, reading between the lines of the Republican leaders' letter, there is an ideological bent, which is actually a thoroughly neoliberal anti-government one. A close look at the situation actually reveals that the Republican letter was driven by their desire to embarrass the government and perhaps push all loan programs to become private-private, thus further coddling a profit-making industry on the backs of students.

Only one conclusion: A real mess

But whether it is the federal government or private lenders, the sheer power of those who loan money to students makes it difficult for struggling borrowers to negotiate flexible repayment plans when they find themselves facing low paying jobs, job loss, wage cuts, or any financial challenges. At this juncture, when individuals default or fall behind on their payments, the blame falls solely on the borrower. In many cases, the public and policymakers do not see how institutions are culpable, or how the forces of nature such as a dire economic recession can impact debtors.

Since there are four main entities—the lenders, the government, the enrollment management cartels, and the universities—plus the financial markets that overlap with all of these areas, it is difficult to explain the full story and make everyone understand that borrowers, and their families, as well as taxpayers, are merely pawns in these larger intertwined systems of power. That is what I am seeking to do here.

Perhaps most startling is the level of corruption by student loan lenders that occurred under George W. Bush's administration. The Department of Education turned a blind eye to this corruption—with the exception of one of its researchers, Dr. Jon Oberg, whose ground-breaking lawsuit will be examined in a subsequent chapter. We'll now turn to the universities themselves, and look closely at the role they play—both the non-profits and for-profits—in participating in the crisis.

Chapter 5
The Complicity
of the Universities

THE LENDING INDUSTRY AS WELL AS THE US government can easily be critiqued as being the culprits behind the student loan debt crisis. The lending industry is culpable for their manipulation of rates and overcharging of students, while the federal government is to blame for the Education Department's inability to properly regulate the private loan industry on behalf of the public.

However, these two bureaucratic institutions aren't the only entities to blame. The universities and colleges, and their problematic relationship to the enrollment management cartels, are another factor in the cataclysmic problems we are facing. Left essentially unregulated, universities—both non-profit and for-profit—have raised, and continue to raise, tuitions whenever they see fit, disproportionately to the rate of inflation or the pricing of other goods and services. The increase in tuition and other fees has been going on for decades, and as everyone knows, many universities charge tuitions that equal buying a new car every year for four years. Since 1978, tuition and other expenditures have gone up over 1100%. Meanwhile, inflation in 1978 was at 7.62% while inflation in 2015 was at 0.12%[25] and since 1978, the total inflation has risen only 368%. In other words, the cost of college has risen about three times the cost of everything else in society.

The corporatization of higher education

Drawing on the "neoliberal" concept of free markets and the notion that everything should be managed according to a profit-seeking model, universities are now run like corporations. These two factors have pushed colleges to become more competitive and even aggressive when seeking to attract students. They have ramped up the stakes to attract the best students (coming from the wealthiest families) by offering the best gym facilities, luxury dorms, and other perks, all the while making the dubious claim that these improvements, which essentially have made many campuses look more like 5–star resorts rather than places of study, are based upon demand.

Furthermore, non-profit universities and colleges are tax exempt. This enormous tax break often causes tensions within the communities in which the schools are situated. Many cities lose substantial tax revenues by being unable to tax the property of universities and colleges in their area. Another source of tension with local communities is related to the fact that these institutions are becoming larger and larger real estate owners in their areas, often gobbling up properties, pushing out families and shopkeepers who have been a part of the neighborhood for decades.

In addition, within the institutions themselves there are built-in tensions based on inequity, given that administrators tend to earn much higher salaries than professors. There are exceptions, depending upon the field, of course, such as professors who become part of the so-called celebrity status, such as Stephen Greenblatt, professor emeritus of English Literature at Harvard and the creator of the school of literary thought known as New Historicism, or full-time faculty members of law and business schools who demand lucrative compensation for speaking or consulting. But overall, these celebrity positions and salaries are few and far between.

Overall, academic power is lopsided, as discussed previously. The administration in most colleges and universities makes most of the decisions, and imposes them in a top-down manner. Even decent salaries for tenured professors are becoming a thing of the past, as tenure track positions are disappearing in favor of hiring "adjunct" professors who are paid far less. Even when a tenured professor retires, the position is not refilled with a new faculty member, but instead, the department hires adjunct faculty. In fact, over 41% of faculty members are adjuncts at colleges and universities today. They have become the new academic proletariat. They carry heavy teaching loads, lack health care, and a growing number of them rely on welfare to make ends meet.

This structural inequity is not without cause. For decades the American university system has deliberately shifted towards a corporate model, utilizing a hierarchical structure of relationships, with administrators, boards, and university presidents consolidating power in a small group of people. This corporate model, at both public and private universities, has also served to undermine the democratic relationships that faculty, as well as the student body, have historically had with administrations. Not only have the former friendly ties been weakened and a top-down model implemented, but the administration has expanded in the number of its highly paid members. These administrators often begin their careers in higher education with a type of technocratic training that in many respects separates them from their peers. There are now M.A. and Ph.D. programs for "Higher Education Administration" to train individuals for management positions within institutions of higher learning. These students are groomed in graduate classrooms with a specific mindset, receiving managerial skills to run schools in a fashion that resembles corporate America.

The evolution of this corporate modeling within academia has run parallel to the changing nature of the student lending industry over the decades. The increasing corporate nature of universities and colleges has, in fact, brought on close ties not just with the student lending industry directly, but also to the financial and banking industry. There are literally overlapping structures of power with varying forms of governance and leadership both within administrations in institutions of higher learning and the student lending industry itself. These structures of power and the individuals who serve as bureaucratic functionaries, at both high and low levels, including even the low-paid customer service representatives for student loan collectors or the student workers in the financial aid offices on college campuses, further perpetuate the system of "Higher Ed Inc." that ultimately relies upon capital—earnings and revenue—which is based predominately on the indebtedness of millions of people to support and upkeep campus building, salaries, maintenance, etc. of our higher education institutions. In short, the universities have as much skin in the student debt loan crisis game as the banks and government agencies that dole out the loans.

Since structures of power are composed of individuals who serve in bureaucratic and technocratic roles, there are, of course, individuals within this system who reap enormous benefits from the corporate model. Their positions of power are often lucrative and fluid. Lawrence Summers, the former director of the National Economic Council under Obama and who was also part of Clinton's administration, is a prime example of this closed loop. Filmmaker Charles Ferguson, who made *Inside Job,* described the former President of Harvard University as an individual who moved easily between "universities, government [positions], and banking."

Not surprisingly, Summers aggressively pushed for extensive deregulation of the banking industry while part of the Clinton administration as Treasury Secretary. Most notable in his work on deregulation was his involvement in the repeal in the Glass-Steagall Act, also known as the Banking Securities Act of 1933. The Glass-Steagall act separated investment banking from commercial banking. This act was passed so that commercial banks would not risk depositors' money in risky investments such as those that sparked the 1929 stock market crash. There is strong evidence that repealing this act under the Clinton Administration led to the 2008 financial crisis that brought world markets to the brink of economic ruin. Summers was not only an academic administrator who moved back and forth between the world of finance and academia, but he also had deep ties to political institutions in Washington.

The frequent movement of people like Summers, the ease with which they move between government, finance, and institutions of higher learning, illustrates the overlap these institutions have with one another. This type of fluidity should not be perceived as coincidental or meaningless. Summers and others like him are able to solidify deep, enduring ties between these institutions of power. To challenge them in a bureaucratic or judicial sense is precarious at best and ruinous at worst.

The student lending industry, of course, has deep, old ties to universities and colleges, but this growing overlap of structural power has played a significant role in how the industry has created tight new linkages among political, financial, and bureaucratic power bases. It is firmly entrenched in political circles in DC and New York financial circles. This structural entrenchment is self-perpetuating and based upon finely cultivated professional relationships, of which Summers is emblematic.

Faculty are pretty much alienated entirely from the ties that the student lending industry has to their institutions. For example, major decisions such as tuition increases and others that result in higher levels of debt for the student body are rarely determined by faculty members. As mentioned, there is a stark economic divide between faculty members and the school administrators. We are looking at a tale of two economic realities, one that in many ways runs parallel to the general trend of rising economic inequality in the US.

Since universities, both private and public, are filling openings previously held by full-time tenured professors with a revolving door of contract-based adjunct workers, a "precariat class" within academia now exists, that is, a class of people who have no security or predictable lifestyles. These adjunct workers lack health benefits and job security. It is difficult for them to unionize for themselves or join up with other employees on campus.

Students are even further marginalized by administrations. For example, a few years ago when students protested tuition hikes within the University of California system, they were resoundingly ignored. This was not the only place where protests against tuition increases have taken place in recent years. Indeed, student protests, especially when Occupy Wall Street (OWS) was organizing events on campuses a few years ago, were numerous and dotted the country. They were not merely about tuition hikes, but they were also in response to the increased corporatization of institutions of higher learning.

A major theme of many protests centered on the fact that college campuses have become less democratic than they had been in the past, especially in how they are led by a managerial elite. Even worse, some of these managerial elite in the financial aid offices not only had direct ties to the student lending industry, but were willing partners in crime when legislation was passed that allowed lenders enormous power over the way in which funders were and continue to be dispersed on college campuses.

Even the nature of public land-grant universities has changed. Many of these state schools no longer invest uniquely in their own in-state residents. Historically, land-grant universities were created in order to serve the populace residing in the state. Instead, land grant universities today often spend a lot of effort to recruit out-of-state and even foreign students so that they can fill their available spots with individuals who will pay higher tuitions.

Sham loan transactions and kickbacks

Universities often have questionable relationships with the student lending industry. The problem is probably more rampant than most of us realize. A prominent example of this was New York Governor Andrew Cuomo's 2007 investigation into Sallie Mae when he was the state's Attorney General. In that case, it was found that financial aid advisors were receiving kickbacks from lenders. Cuomo reached out to 400 colleges across the US, informing them of his investigation. Based upon an in-depth 2007 New York Times article, the investigation found the following illegal activities:

- Lenders paid kickbacks to schools based on a percentage of the loans the financial aid officers directed to the lenders.

- Lenders footed the bills for all-expense-paid trips for financial aid officers to posh resorts and exotic locations. They also provided schools with other benefits like computer systems and put representatives from schools on their advisory boards to curry favors.

- Loan companies set up funds and credit lines for schools to use in exchange for putting lenders on their preferred lender list and offered large payments to schools to drop out of the direct federal loan program so that the lender received more business.

After the case was settled, Sallie Mae said they would no longer offer New York financial aid officers certain perks. But what about similar cases in other states? Was this a pattern? Have other attorney generals been as aggressive as Cuomo in investigating possible wrongdoing by lenders?

While Cuomo might have put a stop to kickbacks and luxurious perks to financial aid officers in New York, recent revelations regarding the lifestyle of NYU's President are worth examining, particularly since that private university is one of the most expensive in the nation. Recently it came to light that loans were being used to purchase mansions for the President of NYU, some of its tops professors, and administrators. A university such as NYU claims they offer such perks in order to retain top talent who would otherwise be lured away to other universities offering them more lucrative salaries and benefits packages.

In June 2013, the New York Times published an article titled, "N.Y.U. Gives Its Stars Loans For Homes," detailing the way in which vacation homes for President John Sexton and others were purchased by money lent by an NYU foundation. The piece was an immediate hit, receiving well over 500 comments. Former alumni, parents with children currently enrolled there, and others were outraged by the article. One reader wrote, "Maybe the top talent could summer in the NYU dorms? My son's freshman dorm had filthy windows, cracked walls, peeling paint and stained bathroom fixtures. I feel like a fool for taking out a federal loan for that!" Another parent wrote, "I have sacrificed tremendously—giving up vacations and more—so my daughter can go to that school. [I]t is outrageous that NYU is giving the administrators forgviable [sic] loans for vacation homes. How can they live in luxury on the backs of their students and the parents that sacrifice for them?"

Others questioned Sexton's justification for such expenses: "Sexton's background is strange. He . . . has an M.A. in comparative religion . . . This sort of background usually emphasizes concerns about ethics, elitism, capitalism and real estate deals." Regardless of Sexton's educational background, the arguments that he and other officials made to justify the expenses on homes should raise troubling doubts in the public mind, as I suggest it is precisely the type of evidence pointing to the corporatization of higher education in America.

Since NYU is a private university, many might argue that the parents and students involved there should have been aware that it is expensive and the students earn a prestigious degree exactly because NYU can attract top professors. Perhaps there is room for debate, but such judgments are unfair for anyone who chooses to attend any institution of higher learning. We all subscribe to the idea that in order to get ahead—particularly economically—we bear a collective responsibility for why young people feel the need to attend college. But to ask these young people to take on debt to support the lavish lifestyles of professors and administrators is beyond logic.

Even those who choose to attend state schools, thinking the choice is reasonable, can wind up deeply in debt given that many state schools are also increasing their tuition. One such example of this problem is the University of California (UC) system, an educational institution that offered at one time very low tuition rates for a world-class education. At one point, the University of California school system was even free. As Charlie Eaton, a PhD candidate in Sociology at UC Berkeley, who studies the politics of higher education finance explains, "California's higher education system has steadily become more unequal over the last 30 years. Today, we educate a smaller share of our state's students in the elite University of California system at a much higher cost per student."

As Eaton points out, a system that was once accessible to the majority of California in-state residents has become a system based upon inequity. He goes on to describe how California's higher education system has experienced what he calls 'revenue shocks' during every recession. "During these revenue shocks, the UC system has increased tuition much more severely than that California State University system or the California community college system, and garnered increasing federal and private research funding."

Beyond twisted tuition: Enrollment management cartels

There is another entity in the murky soup that we must cover in this discussion about the role of the universities in the student loan debt crisis. This is the little known relationship between universities and what are called "enrollment management companies." Many Americans aren't familiar with these operations and the role they play in "Higher Ed Inc."

Enrollment management companies are private firms brought in to oversee financial aid and the admissions process on many campuses across the US. They are deeply connected to a university's brand, and help devise marketing campaigns to attract prospective students. A problematic aspect of their role on campuses is that they often recruit richer students using financial aid packages originally intended for lower-income students, as we discussed in an earlier chapter. One reporter, Matthew Quirk, wrote the following to explain more details about how their game works:

> Financial aid leveraging is the enrollment manager's secret weapon. It has become highly sophisticated since it was first developed, in the 1980s, but the underlying logic remains simple: targeting financial aid will further the interests of the school, typically by bringing in more net revenue or higher-scoring students. Take a $20,000 scholarship — the full tuition for a needy student at some schools. Break it into four scholarships of $5,000 each for wealthier students who would probably go elsewhere without the

discounts but will pay the outstanding tuition if they can be lured to your school. Over four years the school will reap an extra $240,000, which can be used to buy more rich students — or gifted students who will improve the school's profile and thus its desirability and revenue.

The enrollment managers play a large role in the *U.S. News* rankings of the best universities and colleges. In so doing, this elevates a university's brand and thus ranking in that report. This ranking has a troubling relationship to Pell Grants, as policy analyst Steve Burd pointed out:

> [There] is compelling evidence to suggest that many schools are engaged in an elaborate shell game: using Pell Grants to supplant institutional aid they would have provided to financially needy students otherwise, and then shifting these funds to help recruit wealthier students. This is one reason why even after historic increases in Pell Grant funding, the college-going gap between low-income students and their wealthier counterparts remains as wide as ever. Low-income students are not receiving the full benefits intended.
>
> Overall, too many four–year colleges, both public and private, are failing to help government achieve its college access mission. They are, instead, adding hurdles that could hamper the educational progress of needy students, or leave them with mountains of debt after they graduate.

In some cases, these enrollment management companies, which earn fees on the loans they write, use high pressure tactics to get students to agree to loans. One particular case I discovered is that of Marjorie Dillon, who attended Robert

Morris University, and in my view, was misled and placed in the wrong loan program the moment she stepped foot on campus. I wrote about her story in 2009 on my blog, *All Education Matters*, wherein I discussed my attempts to reach out to reporter Tim Grant at the *Pittsburgh Post-Gazette* about his portrayal of Dillon in his article titled, "Student loans put college graduate into deep financial hole." Grant's article largely criticized Dillon for assuming a debt amounting to $120,000, as if it was her fault. He blamed her for her own lack of financial planning, missing federal aid application deadlines, and not meeting academic requirements for federal programs. He cited how Dillon's grandmother co-signed on her loans and how she (the grandmother) was at risk of losing her home, if Dillon, or her co-signer failed to make payments.

At the time, Dillon was a young woman from Coraopolis, Pennsylvania. Various blogs at the time, as well as online comments affixed to Grant's article, expressed sympathy for her. However, others were cutting and cruel (it is the Internet after all). But the cutting, critical, and nasty remarks were not surprising, particularly back in 2008 when the topic was covered so little by mainstream media and outlets like the *Pittsburgh Post-Gazette*.

Though I have no concrete evidence, almost all of these articles on student loan debt, even to this day, still utilize the same type of derogatory language that is eerily the same, formulaic in nature blaming the student for going into debt. This leaves me suspicious that the PR machines from the lenders or other pro-higher education groups have teams of hired personnel to be on the lookout for articles critical of them.

In any event, I was immediately leery of how Tim Grant had written about Dillon in his article. I wanted to know more about the potential role that the financial aid office, along with the enrollment management company hired by Robert Morris University, played in this woman's terrible student loan debt situation. I began my investigation by writing to Grant and suggesting there might be holes in his reporting for blaming her.

I also reached out to Dillon to get clarification of what had happened to her, as I just didn't believe the story added up. I had a hunch that Dillon was taken advantage of by the school as well as by the lender. I did eventually speak to her, and asked her permission to write about her situation, and she granted that to me in 2009.

To make a long story short, Grant's article tried to portray Dillon as having missed many deadlines and lots of facts about her loans that turned out to be false or at least an exaggeration of the truth. His article failed to discuss the enrollment manager who worked for Noel-Levitz, a company that works with students to get loans. (At the time, Noel-Levitz was owned by Sallie Mae.) In my view, no one at the university had actually helped Dillon understand her choices about loans or the amount of debt she would be taking on. It also seems that she was not properly informed that she was eligible for specific loans—Stafford Loans—when she first began taking classes at the university. This fact alone suggests she was poorly advised by the financial aid office about her eligibility for Stafford Loans or other forms of aid under the FAFSA. Chances are, she is not the only one to be victimized. This is all due to the result of inappropriate business relationships between enrollment management companies, lenders, and universities.

There is also a term in enrollment management called "gapped" by which low-income students are intentionally offered far less than what their income requires, in an effort to dissuade them from coming to the school so the institution can use the money for other, wealthier students. The reporter I referred to above, Matthew Quirk, notes, "[some schools] will intentionally gap poor students so severely that they decide not to attend in the first place—or, if they enroll, the long hours of work-study and mounting debts eventually force them to drop out. Called 'admit-deny,' this practice allows a college to keep poor students out while publicly claiming that it doesn't consider a student's finances when making admissions decisions."

Today, I advise low-income students to be aware that they may be ripped off when offered "rotten" financial aid packages by a university that doesn't actually want them to attend. If they don't get the "obvious" message, then it becomes their fault, and they are to blame for foolishly pursuing a degree despite the clearly bad offer given to them at the get-go.

This ruse, on the part of the enrollment management industry, is not only pathologically sick, but is convoluted and even cruel. Again, these facts continue to haunt me and leave me with so many unanswered questions. How many students are being misled, and even ruined by this type of system? And what sort of role does the Department of Education play? Is there anyone within that organization that helps?

The role of for-profit institutions in the crisis

This is a critical last element to discuss in this chapter on the role of universities in creating the student loan debt crisis.

As non-profit colleges and universities increasingly jacked up tuition fees and graduated students whose degrees did not lead to jobs, it was only inevitable that for-profit colleges would begin to take off like wildfire. In many ways, for-profit colleges reflect the thinking of the neoliberal philosophy—privatize education and make money on it. Unfortunately, many of the for-profits have proven to be shams, either granting worthless degrees or in business to lure student loan money to their coffers, or both.

To be clear on definitions, for-profit colleges are privately owned corporations, and often publicly traded. Their programs are often in fields like criminal justice, culinary arts, and other technical fields, meaning they teach subjects that are usually not offered at traditional 4-years colleges and universities.

As for their strong emergence in the last decade, there are a multitude of reasons that they are now a force with which institutions of higher learning must contend. One of these is that they market heavily to convince students that getting a degree at their institution is more valuable than getting a college degree at a typical state university. They use aggressive marketing tactics to target certain groups of students—predominantly older women, African Americans, Hispanics, and low-income individuals, given that they are the ones who typically cannot afford to go to the non-profit universities and colleges.

The for-profits have also taken advantage of recent military veterans, which is another part of this sordid story. I have heard from many soldiers who have returned from war, and their testimonials paint another twisted side to what these schools do to acquire federal funds through shady if not illegal practices using war veterans.

Secondly, as non-profit tuitions have risen, they appear to be a bargain education to students. And with the severe economic downturn, more low-income Americans and minorities have turned to for-profits for additional training and education, only to be driven further into debt, often while obtaining dubious degrees that lead to low-paying jobs or dead ends.

In addition, they often advertise aggressively that they will help students obtain loans to pay for their tuition—and as a result they have become a major culprit in manipulating the federal government's student loans to their coffers. Indeed, for-profits institutions, between 2010 and 2011, received $32 billion in taxpayer money. Much of this money went towards paying for enormous salaries of the presidents, administrative staff, and marketing teams. It's not surprising that for-profit schools pay their administrators exorbitant salaries. The enormously inflated salaries, bonuses, and perks of for-profit college presidents make the salaries of non-profit presidents appear meager. Even the President of Harvard, only earned about $900,000 in 2011 while most for-profit university presidents earn well over $1 million a year.

The power of the for-profits began building up when President George W. Bush was in office. The loosening of federal funds allowed the for-profits to take full advantage of taxpayers' dollars spent on student loans.

However, as their power mounted, more and more cases of for-profit schools using false advertising were discovered, and they came under scrutiny. In 2010, for instance, the GAO investigated fifteen for-profits across the country. Their findings revealed that these schools engaged in fraudulent practices to both obtain federal loan money directed to them, and to persuade students that their degrees were worth investing in. A report the GAO published, entitled, "For-Profit Colleges: Undercover Tooting Finds Colleges Encouraged Fraud and Engaged in Deceptive and Questionable Marketing," stated the following:

Undercover tests at 15 for-profit colleges found that 4 colleges encouraged fraudulent practices and that all 15 made deceptive or otherwise questionable statements to GAO's undercover applicants. Four undercover applicants were encouraged by college personnel to falsify their financial aid forms to qualify for federal aid—for example, one admissions representative told an applicant to fraudulently remove $250,000 in savings. Other college representatives exaggerated undercover applicants' potential salary after graduation and failed to provide clear information about the college's program duration, costs, or graduate rate despite federal regulations requiring them to do so. For example, staff commonly told GAO's applicants they would attend classes for 12 months a year, but stated the annual cost of attendance for 9 months of classes, misleading applicants about the total cost of tuition. Admissions staff used other deceptive practices, such as pressuring applicants to sign a contract for enrollment before allowing them to speak to a financial aid advisor about program cost and financing options.

Another investigation into for-profits was revealed to me by David Goodstein, a former employee of Kaplan College in Pennsylvania. Goodstein came to me with his story about one of Kaplan's campuses in Pennsylvania several years ago. He alleged that the school lured students into signing up for a surgical-technology program that literally had no capability to be completed. That is, the program literally could *not* graduate all students because it lacked enough externships at hospitals that students had to have had to get their degree. The students were thus defrauded, and had no degrees to show for the work they had done. Furthermore, many of the students had federal government loans, so the school was also defrauding the government.

Goodstein, a high-ranking employee at Kaplan, was incensed by the situation and took action by becoming a whistleblower and reporting the fraud. The US Department of Justice agreed with him, and in 2011 a lawsuit was settled with the government for $1.6 million.

In this case, the whistleblower and the students won in court, but what about the millions of other students who now attend for-profits, and then drop-out when they realize their programs will not lead to real jobs, yet they still face huge debts to pay for the courses they took under false pretenses? Unfortunately, for many, their lives, and the lives of their family members, are destroyed financially and emotionally as a result of becoming indebted for life.

In 2012, Former Senator Tom Harkin (D-IA) also published a scathing report documenting abuses in the for-profit education industry. The Obama administration also attempted to put a halt to the growth of spurious for-profit colleges, with the "Gainful Employment Rule" which was introduced in June of 2011 and was intended to put a stop to all the shenanigans of for-profits. In an official press release, the Education Department stated:

Today, the Obama Administration released final regulations requiring career college programs to better prepare students for 'gainful employment' or risk losing access to Federal student aid. While many career college programs are helping to prepare America's workforce for jobs of the future, far too many students at these schools are taking on unsustainable debt in exchange for degrees and certificates that fail to help them get jobs they need or were promised. These regulations are designed to ramp up over the next four years, giving colleges time to reform while protecting students and their families from exploitative programs.

Secretary of Education Arne Duncan also weighed in, stating, "These new regulations will help ensure that students at these schools are getting what they pay for: solid preparation for a good job." He added, "We're giving career colleges every opportunity to reform themselves but we're not letting them off the hook, because too many vulnerable students are being hurt."

However, with the announcement of the Gainful Employment Ruling, there was immediate pushback from the proprietary schools, which were and continue to be enormously powerful in DC (though with all this scrutiny, these schools, thankfully, have taken some hits). Their lobbying worked, as officials within government ranks began taking a stance against treating the for-profits so harshly, probably in exchange for campaign donations. For instance, House Education Committee Chairman John Kline (R-MN) saw a significant increase in donations to his election campaign from for-profit colleges in the summer of 2013. Not surprisingly, he later pushed through legislation that would help the for-profit industry preserve its access to federal student loans.

As David Halperin, an attorney and writer for RepublicReport.org, noted, Kline's spuriously named bill, Supporting Academic Freedom through Regulatory Relief Act, "has nothing to do with actual academic freedom. Instead, Kline's bill is about blocking the Obama administration from issuing the new 'gainful employment' rule that would have ended tax-payer support for career training programs that consistently leave students with insurmountable loan debt. The bill was also about relaxing federal standards so for-profit college boiler room operations can more easily engage in coercive recruiting students."

Even Eduardo Ochoa, assistant secretary for postsecond-ary education at the US Education Department, intimated that the final legislation of the Gainful Employment Rul-ing would probably not be all that disconcerting to the for-profits. He said, "The regulations as they come out are going to be significantly different—I think they're going to be better, nuanced, and I think that there's a lot there that people will appreciate having other views reflected."

The message was clear. When someone in a high position such as Eduardo Ochoa uses words like "nuanced," it is code for the following: "we've been lobbied and pressured so hard that we're going to cave to the demands of the for-profit indus-try." As it turns out, the schools that should have been regu-lated by the Department wound up drafting the new rules for themselves! The administration backed off from the propri-etary schools and in the end took no measures to tackle the ever growing student lending crisis.

While in the past, these for-profits were largely ignored by the university community as well as by policymakers for years, they have become a significant force in higher education. Most troubling about this shift and growing recognition of the for-profits is the manner in which higher education policy circles have even contributed to legitimizing them through convo-luted academic discourse. Even more problematic, there are now partnerships popping up between traditional universities and for-profits. This is yet another reason to suggest that all of these schools are part of a systemic crisis, regardless of what category they happen to fall under. The rise of the for-profits overlaps with the neoliberal economic model.

Today, as I write, most of the for-profits still thrive, driven by the myth they propagate that feeds the American dream of getting a diploma from an institution of advanced learning. It is sad but probably true that the for-profit sector is likely to be a key beneficiary of President Obama's $12 billion plan to produce five million more two-year college graduates over the next decade. While some of these students may earn viable degrees that lead to jobs, the evidence now suggests that many will face a dead-end, with questionable diplomas and low-income job prospects.

Chapter 6
The Agencies, the Bureaucrats, and the Politicians

THE DEPARTMENT OF EDUCATION HAS PLAYED A significant role in the student loan debt crisis, too. While they have implemented some beneficent programs like ICR (Income Contingent Repayment Program), IBR (Income Based Repayment), an updated version of REPAYE (Revised Pay As You Earn), and other related forgiveness programs, the Department is far more oriented towards supporting an army of collectors who have received favorable contracts to track down delinquent borrowers or those who have defaulted on their federal student loans. This has created a system in which an entire industry, the student debt collection industry, has emerged and greatly benefited, particularly during times of economic downturns.

In 2012, student loan debt collectors earned $51 billion for the Department, a figure higher than Exxon Mobil which earned $44.9 billion in 2012 and about the same as four major banks—Wells Fargo, Bank of America, JP Morgan Chase, and Citigroup, which together made profits of $51.9 billion. The Department's collections, based upon the Congressional Budget Office, were also forecast to jump precipitously starting in 2015 up to an estimated $127 billion in the next 10 years.[26]

And while there are purportedly all of these loan forgiveness programs and a current Democrat in the White House, the total student loan debt has doubled since Obama took office, and the collectors are out in force. What might this mean? My answer: the government, along with the industry that is not only allowed to exist but thrive, also profits from long-term student loan debt.

The collectors, some of whom had also been previously originators of loans, continue to do well as a result of government contracts won through bids with the Department of Education. Furthermore, many individual collectors have pocketed tremendous amounts of cash. One collector, for example, named Joshua Mandelman who resided in Minnesota, earned $454,000 chasing student loan debtors, as reporter John Hechinger detailed in a shocking 2012 article.[27] Mandelman's boss Richard Boyle, earned $1.1 million in 2010. The two men worked for a corporation called Educational Credit Management Corporation (ECMC). Referred to as a guaranty agency, it is among many players who add yet another level of complexity to the student lending industry.

There are 32 guaranty agencies that operate as an offshoot, a tool of sorts, of the Department of Education. Essentially, they guarantee loans by banks and other entities. If a borrower stops paying on these guaranteed loans to them, these agencies pay back the loans. However, if the agencies are unable to recoup the money owed, the problem is no longer theirs. It becomes a problem for taxpayers, as the issue is then turned over to the federal government.

Thus the current system rewards collection agencies with money from taxpayers when student borrowers default. This bureaucratic and financial relationship to these guaranty agencies don't seem to be of benefit to borrowers or taxpayers. After Hechinger's article was written, the Obama administration revisited the profits being made by the collection agencies, and lowered the commission rates for collectors going after borrowers with delinquent loans. But this has been only a small step to fix a problem, compared to the amounts of money that guaranty agencies are earning from student debtors and the federal government.

Only recently, the well-known student-loan ombudsman formerly at the Consumer Financial Protection Bureau (CFPB), Rohit Chopra, joined the Department of Education. He has been an ally of borrowers and was a harsh critic of both the Obama administration and the Department of Education. Perhaps with Chopra working for the Department, these enormous institutional issues that relate to the guaranty agencies will be further scrutinized and eventually changed from within.

But even with individuals willing to scrutinize the Department of Education like Chopra, and political leaders such as Senator Elizabeth Warren (who, incidentally, helped create the CFPB) and Presidential candidate Bernie Sanders, the public is up against powerful interest groups and lobbyists representing the student lending industry as well as the universities and colleges. Furthermore, there exists parasitic relationships between the Department and the lenders.

While many Americans are now familiar with the scandalous activities of Wall Street, few are aware of a case that a former bureaucrat and Department of Education researcher, Dr. Jon Oberg, brought against the lenders on behalf of American taxpayers and the US government. This legal case, which highlights Oberg's heroism as a "mere" government bureaucrat, is an example of the way in which good bureaucrats try to expose corruption and illegal activity within the government. Getting to the root of systemic corruption is no easy task, as it is often difficult to point fingers at specific culprits—even when they do exist—and the crime scenes can be so large, inhabiting boring bureaucratic landscapes—piles of paperwork, electronic emails, labyrinthine cables that connect databases to other databases. The criminals often appear flawless; they are neatly dressed bureaucrats who move in and out of these circles easily, all the while committing financial crimes of enormous magnitude. Often when their systemic criminal activity is discovered by someone like Oberg, it is too late or the crime is too big for the public to even digest. That is why this story needs to be told here. This story is known as the 9.5% loophole scandal.

Dr. Jon Oberg discovers the 9.5% loophole scandal

Most people among the American public are unaware of the 9.5% loophole scandal, but it is well known in the education and political circles in DC as well as among higher education policy analysts, such as Steve Burd at the New America Foundation, who revealed and discussed it in detail as it was unfolding. Historian Tim Lacy also provided insights into this case on his blog Thinking Through History. Labeling it a loophole, however, belies what Oberg actually found. Through exhaustive and scrupulous research, Oberg found that specific players involved stole money directly from the US Treasury.

Who exactly is Oberg, and what did he expose about outright theft that was carried out by some of the biggest lenders in the industry? Oberg was a bureaucrat and researcher at the Department of Education who discovered that a number of major lenders were defrauding taxpayers. These lenders stole upwards of $1 billion from the US Treasury.

The story began in the 1990s. At the time Oberg was the Education Department liaison to Congress. While in this role, he uncovered that non-profit lenders were taking advantage of an archaic lending system based upon subsidies from a 1980s student lending structure. As a result, the lenders were receiving, through a form of bureaucratic manipulation, subsidies that they shouldn't have been receiving. These acts of obtaining the subsidies in this way were being done deliberately.

In 1997, Oberg approached Sally Stroup, who at the time was a senior aide to the Republican Chairman of the House Education Committee. Around the same time, the Clinton administration tried to put an end to these subsidies through legislation via the Higher Education Act. Stroup essentially told Oberg that it would be impossible to include any verbiage to fix the loophole in the reauthorization of that act.

Undeterred by Stroup's refusal, Oberg soon had an opportunity to do even more digging into what he suspected were illegal activities. In 2000, he was transferred to a research division at the Department of Education, where he discovered, through extensive investigatory research, that this so-called loophole was outright theft. They were "gaming the system," Oberg told New York Times reporter Sam Dillon in an article published in 2007 after the case came to light.

After collecting more than enough proof in 2003, Oberg approached Grover Whitehurst, a political appointee in the George W. Bush administration. He was once again instructed to drop it, and to work on other projects after he presented his findings. In one email from Whitehurst, as noted in the 2007 article by Dillon, Oberg was told, "In the 18 months you have remaining, I will expect your time and talents to be directed primarily to our business of conceptualizing, competing and monitoring research grants." The theft continued despite what Oberg had revealed to Whitehurst. Despite identifying a clear pattern of abuse, he was effectively told to shut up.

The theft continued for three more years. Oberg made it clear that he was worried that "student lending companies were improperly collecting hundreds of millions of federal subsidies." Moreover, he said, "[I] suggested how to correct the problem." What was the Department's excuse for ignoring this egregious theft? They insisted that there was nothing they could do about the overpayments on outdated subsidies, and concluded that it was a matter with which Congress needed to change through legislation.

Once Oberg retired—he was most likely forced into early retirement—he decided that he could not remain silent. So, in 2009 Oberg filed a lawsuit in the United State District Court for the Eastern District of Virginia, Alexandria Division, against several student loan companies, including the three largest ones: Sallie Mae, Nelnet, and PHEAA. Not surprisingly, Sallie Mae immediately claimed that it took no part in the 9.5 percent student loan scheme. What was Oberg seeking? As reported by the *Chronicle of Higher Education*, Oberg sought "the return of $1-billion in excess of student-loan subsidies to the federal government."

As litigation began against the lenders, damning evidence appeared in the court documents. In one place, for example, a lender scrawled on a document, 'God Bless George Dubya

Bush!" for overlooking activity that was clearly fraudulent. Part of the suit has already been settled, and Oberg won $55 million, the bulk of which went back to the US government. However, not all lenders have settled, and the case remains under litigation.

Those who turned a blind eye or were directly involved with this criminal activity have paid no price. For example, Sally Stroup, once she was done being a bureaucrat in various roles in DC, including time spent at the Department of Education, became the director of government and industry affairs for the Apollo Group, Inc./University of Phoenix from 1993 to 2001. Stroup's story is common, a classic case of the revolving door between high-level bureaucratic positions at the Department of Education and industry, in this case the for-profit or proprietary schools, fraught with scandal. While Stroup did not commit a crime, she appeared to block Oberg's attempts to right a clear wrong. This has had no impact upon her career to this day.[28]

Most recently, Stroup was the Executive Vice President of Government Relations and General Counsel to the Association for Private Sector Colleges and Universities (APSCU). APSCU in recent years has fought to destroy the Obama administration's attempts to hold for-profit schools accountable through proof of gainful employment after their students graduate.[29] As for Grover Whitehurst, he now holds a position at the Brookings Institution. While these two individuals were not concerned with specific outcomes relating to taxpayers, Oberg illustrates the power of what one good bureaucrat can do when systemic corruption is discovered.

Moreover, with news that the former student-loan ombudsman Rohit Chopra from CFPB has moved over to the

Department of Education, a new Student Aid Enforcement Unit to investigate fraud has been launched. Along with the recent appointment of Ted Mitchell as Undersecretary, there is now hope that the institution and individual players within it who had a tendency to be more oriented towards lenders and collectors than student debtors will change.

The politicians

Most of the American public is well aware that politicians receive money from the banks, oil companies, and powerful lobbying groups who support specific industry initiatives. So, it should come as no surprise that politicians also receive donations and financial support from the banking industry, from the for-profit and non-profit schools, and from the associations who represent them, and from the lenders. This is, of course, a given in the American political structure. Thus, it is safe to conclude that there are a lot of politicians who are not looking out for the interests of prospective students, current student borrowers in school, or those of us who graduated with existing debt. If one listens carefully to their rhetoric, it becomes clear as to who is filling their campaign coffers.

For example, Representative Virginia Fox (R-NC), who is the current chair of the Higher Education Subcommittee, has received ample support from the for-profit education industry. She is just one of many representatives who are on influential committees, and she makes it a point to cater to the interests of the lobbying groups who drive "Higher Ed Inc." Their allegiances are revealed in the way in which they vote on legislation that affects funding for higher education and student loan borrowers, and on what they say about the student loan crisis. A few years ago, for instance, Foxx told an interviewer that she had "little tolerance" for people with student loan debt. After she made this remark, she was quickly chastised by President Obama. She shot back, insisting that the President misconstrued her remarks. She went on to claim that she was only critical of people who graduated with $80,000 in student loan debt or more. A bit absurd, in my book. (By the way, the figure chosen — $80,000 — is an interesting one because Foxx graduated from the University of North Carolina in 1961 when tuition was approximately $87.50 per semester. If that were adjusted for inflation, it would amount to just $660 per semester in today's dollars. What does the University of North Carolina cost now though? According to the University's website, the average cost per year to attend is around $20,000. That means that students who borrow their full college costs now would graduate from Foxx's alma mater with $80,000 in debt.)

Not only is it disconcerting that Foxx seems to lack compassion for the dramatic spike in the cost of tuition and other fees to attend a 4-year university in the US, but it is problematic that she is chair of the Higher Education Subcommittee. She is not the only politician who has been bought by the student lending industry, but she is noteworthy given her position of power on a particular subcommittee that deals with higher education issues.

Fortunately, there is a counterbalance to politicians like Foxx, the most notable being Senator Elizabeth Warren (D-MA). Warren is a huge champion of distressed borrowers, and thus is in need of our support. And there are others worth mentioning. Senator Sherrod Brown (D-OH) is another ally of ours. Over the many years that he has been on the Hill, he has proposed legislation that would help distressed borrowers. Most recently, he proposed legislation for a student loan debt swap. If this had passed, the federal government would have assumed ownership over private loans, making the repayment plans more flexible than under the private loan sector.

There is also the former Senator from Iowa, Tom Harkin, who led investigations into the for-profit industry. These investigations were not good for him politically; he received a lot of heat from the for-profits and their lobbyists. He was also roundly attacked by think thanks that were pro-business and defended the for-profit schools. Regardless of this uphill battle, Harkin continued with his investigations. His presence, as an ally for student debtors, is missed.

Senators Dick Durbin (D-IL) and Al Franken (D-MN) have both made efforts to restore bankruptcy protections to borrowers. Their efforts also deserve acknowledgment. Finally, there is Presidential candidate Bernie Sanders, whose ideas will be discussed in more detail in the next chapter.

This is a short list of political leaders who are compassionate and aware of the student loan debt crisis. But focusing on those who can make a difference and push for changes, along with bureaucrats such as Oberg, Chopra, and Mitchell, there still remains the possibility for policy changes that could help bring relief to the 43 million Americans who have student loan debt.

In my final chapter, I will discuss seven solutions that address both policymakers and the public. While this crisis is unprecedented and daunting, there are a multitude of ways in which it could be fixed now. We don't have to wait, and we shouldn't have to wait.

Chapter 7
Seven Solutions to Solve the Student Debt Crisis

WE CAN NO LONGER DOWNPLAY THE PROBLEM. It has been clearly established that there is a student loan debt crisis. The problem is being discussed by politicians on both sides of the aisle; it is mentioned frequently in the press; and increasingly it has become a topic of conversation at the dinner tables of American families, especially for those with kids who have yet to go to college and for those whose graduates have been forced to move back home because of the burden of their monthly student loan debt payments. It's also become a topic of discussion in the 2016 presidential election.

When I first began to write about the issue and advocate on behalf of the millions of people with student loan debt, no one anywhere, not even on Capitol Hill, was discussing this crisis, despite the fact that it was already out of hand.

That is no longer the case. We have finally come to accept that we have a crisis on our hands. But since we have agreed that there is a problem—a serious one of great magnitude to the tune of $1.3 trillion—we need to move towards productive discussions that lead to solutions with tangible results for past borrowers still deep in debt, as well as for future borrowers. These solutions must also address the entire enterprise of "Higher Education Inc." in the context of refashioning the way America educates our youth through college and university degrees. This refashioning also relates to the reconceptualization of higher education as a public good again, not merely considering it job training for people to have just so they can be "marketable" in a capitalist-driven job market.

This chapter offers seven solutions. Admittedly, some are idealistic, but most of them are pragmatic and could be easily implemented. Some of these solutions are intended for policymakers and political leaders, while others are directed towards prospective students, current borrowers, and parents who want to help their children make informed decisions or those who are borrowing on their children's behalf. The seven solutions are as follows:

1. Debt Jubilee, the total wiping out of student debt for all student loan debtors
2. Free public university education for all
3. Making IBR (Income Based Repayment) after forgiveness of 20 years non-taxable/bill-free
4. Offering options to refinance student loans
5. Reestablishing bankruptcy protection rights to borrowers for both private and federal loans
6. Tackling the crisis at the state level, especially by offering free community college but also by aiding prospective, current, and distressed borrowers

7. Actively supporting politicians who fight on behalf of borrowers and students

Let's review each of these.

Implement a debt jubilee

Debt Jubilees are from ancient times, with references to them even in the Bible. When a debt jubilee occurs, all debts are wiped away and debtors receive a clean slate. This concept, unfortunately for debtors, has been lost on the modern world, although Iceland recently experimented with it.

I have called for a debt jubilee on student debt in the past, but my ideas differ from an earlier movement related to "forgiving student loan debt" that appeared prior to the Occupy Wall Street days. The reason is that I find the language relating to "forgiveness" problematic. Thanks to the way legislation has been written and the power that the student lending industry possesses, it makes little sense to approach the titans on bended knee. After all, it wasn't the borrowers who created this mess, so it really raises the question of who should be forgiving whom? The answer seems to be those who wield the power, and that certainly is not the borrowers or the parents of borrowers.

Aside from the language issue, a debt jubilee would be a splendid way to reboot the economy, to immediately help *all* student loan borrowers. They would NO longer be debtors! The positive repercussions are almost unthinkable for everyone, including taxpayers who are also part of this trap that has been caused by this systemic crisis. After all, when the banks nearly brought the global economy to its knees in 2008, we—the taxpayers—bailed them out, so why not bail out Americans who went to school in order to contribute to

American society? The payoffs might be tremendous, both economically and most certainly psychologically.

Since I mentioned Occupy Wall Street and its call for a debt jubilee, let me discuss that here in slightly more detail. In November of 2011 a collective called the Occupy Student Loan Debt Campaign sprang out of the Occupy Wall Street movement, and it ran until spring of 2012. The movement was a coalition of people who then formed a project called "Strike Debt" in the summer of 2012. The formation of this group centered around the particular theme of protesting student loan debt. This movement provided a space for student debtors and faculty members like Andrew Ross, a Professor in the Department of Social and Cultural Analysis at NYU, to air their grievances and denounce the predatory lending system that makes up the student loan debt industry.

As Pamela Brown, another spokesperson for the Occupy Student Loan Debt Campaign, made clear, "We believe our political system is dysfunctional because it has been taken over by corporations and the 1%. We believe that nonviolent direct action is the only way to transform higher education which has become a site of enormous bank profits and a critical juncture in the production of extreme inequality. We do not believe that petitioning a corrupt government will have an impact."

That sentiment, for numerous reasons, deepened as more OWS protesters hit the streets. It was not just about expressing grievances. It sought change, too. The group's original political operations urged student loan debtors to engage in a collective strike, a refusal to pay, in order to fight against the lenders. Basing the refusal to pay on union strikes—the last option left on the table when disputes between unions and management have stagnated or failed—the group tried to come up with a way to use this as a model for student loan debtors.

Later there was also the Debt Collective, which emerged out of Debt Strike and helped organize the "Corinthian 15." This group of 15 students were organized as a sort of union concept by Debt Strike. They attended programs run by a for-profit known as Corinthian Colleges. The school(s) collapsed and the students were left deeply in debt. The Consumer Financial Protection Bureau (CFPB) investigated Corinthian Colleges, concluding that its lending practices were predatory. These 15 debtors demanded that the Department of Education use its authority to forgive their debt. The group now has over 100 borrowers demanding their debts be forgiven. They have had enough leverage to even hold meetings with top members at the Department of Education.

Even though OWS has long since passed, the streets now empty and the camp sites gone, the majority of Americans feel that the government is against them, and are only interested in supporting corporations and those individuals with influence, power, and enormous coffers. This cynicism and sentiment runs across the political spectrum. OWS was a place where many believed collective action took place. Within this space it became possible to denounce the student lending industry, along with the universities, and name those who have taken advantage of the system and turned educated Americans into permanent debtors. As Meister noted, it was up to the debtors to seize the opportunity and reclaim things that had been taken from them; their dignity, their freedom, and even their educated minds. This was also a space to rethink what our democratic institutions should be doing for us as citizens. It also allows us to rethink the possibilities of reclaiming governmental institutions to serve our purposes as citizens, rather than dismantling or abandoning these institutions that belong to us.

Offer free public universities

There has already been talk about making 2-year community colleges free, an idea that makes sense, considering their low cost of tuitions to attend. Bernie Sanders has taken that idea a step further, calling for free public college all the way through 4-year institutions. This option is not so absurd as some might think. As already noted in prior chapters, not so long ago in US history, college was practically free—such as in California and New York. In an op-ed published in October 2015, Sanders expressed his reasons for why public university should be free:

> In my view, education is essential for personal and national well-being. We live in a highly competitive, global economy, and if our economy is to be strong, we need the best-educated workforce in the world. We won't achieve that if, every year, hundreds of thousands of bright young people cannot afford to go to college while millions more leave school deeply in debt. We need to ensure that every young person in this country who wishes to go to college can get the education that he or she desires, without going into debt and regardless of his or her family's income.

A large number of schools throughout nations in Europe such as Finland, Sweden, Norway, Denmark, Germany, as well as in Mexico, offer free higher education. Germany has even encouraged US students to apply to their universities, where they can go for free. Their motivation: Germany is hoping to attract the top talent of the world. Dorothea Rueland, secretary general of the German Academic Exchange Service (known in Germany as its acronym DAAD), believes that educating people for free makes sense. She points out that half of the students they attract to German universities who graduate make Germany their home and 40 percent of them stay for at least 10 years, compared to only 12 percent of foreign students in the US. "We depend on innovation, on inventions—and where do they come from? From institutions of higher education or from research institutions," Rueland points out. She also adds, "If you look at the global challenges everybody's talking about, questions of climate change, energy, water, high-tech ... this cannot be solved by one institution or one country. So you have to have international networks."

Bernie Sanders is actually concerned about the number of students who leave each year to study in Germany. "That's why every year, more than 4,600 students leave the United States and enroll in German universities. For a token fee of about $200 per year, an American can earn a degree in math or engineering from one of the premier universities in Europe." Keeping in mind what Rueland said about foreign students staying in Germany after they graduate, it is likely that the US is losing half of these students to Germany each year. That is a clear cut case of brain drain as a direct result of the student loan debt crisis in the US.

Funding students at higher education institutions spurs economic growth, innovation, and entrepreneurialism. Sanders sums up the argument in an irrefutable way: "Governments in these countries [who fund higher education] understand what an important investment they are making, not just in the individuals who are able to acquire knowledge and skills but for the societies these students will serve as teachers, architects, scientists, entrepreneurs and more."[30]

Make IBR (Income Based Repayment) after forgiveness of 20 years non-taxable and bill-free

When Income Based Repayment (IBR) was implemented, initially loan forgiveness was offered only after 25 years. Loan forgiveness is now offered after 20 years. IBR was also incorporated with Public Service Loan Forgiveness (PSLF), meaning that if individuals went into careers in the public service — non-profit organizations, a wide range of government work/entities, serving in the Peace Corps or Ameri-Corps full-time — their payments would be lowered.

IBR also allows people to stop paying their loans entirely in the event they become unemployed. There is, however, a catch. Consider the following scenario. Let's say an individual went to a state university and took out loans for four years to graduate. According to the College Board, the average cost of going to a 4-year public university is $9,410. That figure is an *average,* however. Millions of Americans do not pay the average when it comes to their loans, but are above the average, well above the average, or dangerously above the average.

But let's use average costs, for the sake of argument. If a student graduates on time, the total amount for an undergraduate degree on average would be $37,640—a pretty hefty burden of debt for a new graduate. Chances are the job market is weak and highly competitive. Perhaps the student, who is now a borrower, is able to find work, but only here and there. So the borrower opts to enroll in the IBR program. Upon entering, let's say something occurs that makes it impossible for the borrower to work again. After 20 years, the loan is forgiven, which means the borrower has nothing to worry about, right? Wrong. After adding in accrued interest for the amount not paid, the student could owe far more than the original $37,640. The borrower will then receive a tax bill from the IRS, as the remaining money owed is considered a taxable gift. This could amount to a few thousand dollars in taxes owed.

There is no reason for this stipulation to exist; it adds more burden to the student who could not even pay the loan. I have spoken to staffers who work for Democrats and Republicans, and we all agree: this stipulation is a problem and needs to be changed.

Enable debtors to refinance loans at lower interest rates

Numerous Democrats have been pushing for this solution in recent years—allowing debtors to refinance high interest loans into lower interest ones. When President Obama delivered his final State of the Union Address in January, 2016, several Congressional leaders, including Senator Debbie Stabenow (D-MI), wore red buttons that read: "Students: #InTheRed." This campaign was launched by Higher Ed, Not Debt, a group organized by the Center for American Progress. Moreover, the campaign encouraged student debtors to use the hashtag #InTheRed to send out tweets during the State of the Union Address.

Refinancing federal loans at lower rates is a meaningful and pragmatic way to help with higher education financial reform. It would help millions who are already part of the student debtor class. And it makes as much sense as allowing home owners to refinance a mortgage if a lower rate is available. It is simply not understandable why this option is not available for student loan borrowers as well. The results might even change the behavior of the lenders, making them realize they must actually compete for borrowers and keep them as satisfied customers, or risk the losing their business to another lender.

Reestablish bankruptcy protection rights for borrowers

Bankruptcy protection rights were gradually stripped from borrowers, beginning with federal loans and then with private loans, the latter of which occurred under the second Bush administration. The reasons for stripping borrowers of these protections were based upon claims that scores of doctors and lawyers, who simply had no interest in paying back their student loan debt, quickly declared bankruptcy right after graduating with their degrees. While there might have been a few cases of this in the late 1970s and early 1980s, the assertion that a multitude of such professionals were doing it has been proven false.

Nevertheless, the suspicion still led policymakers to pass punitive measures, thus eventually making it impossible to discharge student loan debt of any kind—federal or private—in bankruptcy. These draconian laws need to be changed, and should have been changed long ago. Restoring bankruptcy protection rights to student borrowers needs to happen immediately.

There are two audiences who need to consider the arguments about this issue. The first are the policymakers in DC, for whom reestablishing bankruptcy protection rights to borrowers has been debated on Capitol Hill for quite some time. The attempts to reinstate consumer protections for student borrowers has been pushed through various pieces of legislation in recent years on the Hill. Political leaders have also urged the Department of Education to reconsider bankruptcy laws. In 2011, Senators Sheldon Whitehouse (D-RI) and Al

Franken (D-MN) along with Representatives Steve Cohen (D-TN), Danny Davis (D-IL), George Miller (D-CA) and John Conyers (D-MI) tried to introduce legislation that would have allowed for the discharging of private student loan debt in bankruptcy.[31] The legislation failed. In May of 2014, Representative Steve Cohen (D-TN), along with several Democratic senators, encouraged Secretary of Education Arne Duncan to reconsider the criteria that make distressed borrowers eligible for discharging their federal loans in bankruptcy.

These are just two of countless examples of efforts to do something about this solution to student loan debt. Numerous political leaders in office agree that bringing back those protections is not only necessary but imperative. This issue should be considered a top priority, and restoring bankruptcy protection rights should be just one of many ways in which to address the student loan debt crisis. Furthermore, legislation introduced should include the ability to discharge *both* federal and private loans.

The second audience I want to address are prospective borrowers, the parents of prospective borrowers, as well as individuals who are considering co-signing on student loans or taking out Parent PLUS loans. To reiterate, it is nearly impossible to discharge student loan debt in bankruptcy, so beware of what you are signing or co-signing. If the primary borrower is unable to pay their debts (private loans), those loans become the secondary borrower's 100% responsibility. Lenders do not see them in a different category. In a word, they are stuck footing the *entire* bill.

There is an option for Total and Permanent Discharge (TPD) of federal loans due to disability, but the actual process is difficult, even after debilitating health problems or a severe injury.[32] The same goes with discharging private loans.[33]

Third, those who take out Parent PLUS loans should be aware of the numerous dangers involved. First, it is additional debt added to the parent's debt portfolio. Second, if something catastrophic occurs to the borrower, such as death, and the Parent PLUS loan is discharged, the IRS will attempt to tax the discharged amount as a function of debt income. This is known as a 1099-C. If a borrower receives a 1099-C as a result of loans being discharged, it is in their best interest to seek advice from a tax advisor. Borrowers need to be aware of these harsh realities. To his credit, President Obama introduced relief to these borrowers in his last and final budget plan in February of 2016. But whether or not Congress does anything to implement it remains to be seen.

The state-level approach to solving the crisis

Since there is considerable gridlock at the national level, there are still possibilities to solve the student loan debt crisis at the state level. In fact, there are already groups approaching the problem in this way, thus avoiding the ideological drama occurring in DC. One particular organization, The Campaign for Free College, which aims to make community colleges in the US free, quickly realized that a state level approach made more sense than implementing a policy plan at the federal level. I spoke to Morley Winograd, the founder of the Campaign for Free College Tuition about the group's decision to take this route. Originally, the group wanted to disburse loans to make pubic college tuition free through National Promise Scholarships. Winograd told me that the disbursement would have originally been through the federal government. The plan even had bipartisan support. But despite this support Winograd and his colleagues soon realized that the plan would fail in Congress. As he told me, "The chances of having it listened to, let alone heard, in Congress were practically nil."

That's when they came up with a new alternative: the state level approach. Winograd is happy to report, "[a]lready two states, one with Republican leadership and one with Democratic, have enacted free community college tuition for their residents, and many more are actively debating the idea. It is clear that these state leaders, especially governors, need to take a much more practical and less ideological approach to ideas that can help solve the very real problems their constituencies are having."

Thus, we have a clear example of how state level initiatives can lead to policies that have a direct impact upon issues that relate to the student loan debt crisis. Furthermore, it is reasonable to assume that current students aren't the only group who could benefit from approaching the crisis at the state level. Certainly policymakers, with engaged groups acting on behalf of distressed borrowers, could also implement policies to offer immediate relief as well. For example, there could be ways in which bankruptcy protections could work through exemptions, as such laws in Kansas exist for land. Perhaps this sort of approach could be applied to garnishment rules. The challenge would be with federal loans, as federal government laws always trump state laws. Nevertheless, this might be a way in which advocates could try to tackle the issue for distressed borrowers. So, there could be garnishment rules as well as exemptions and those could be enlarged beyond the ones that relate to houses or cars. (There could also be a "guerrilla tactic" by which attorneys who represent distressed borrowers could strike out language that is highly punitive, so that when it does go to court, the contracts have been altered in favor of the debtor. Even borrowers could implement this type of approach with the contract). On a side note, distressed borrowers should be aware that in many states there are legal aid organizations that specialize in student loan law. For example, the National Consumer Law Center (NCLC) based in Boston, Massachusetts, does excellent work on behalf of distressed borrowers. They also have a robust website (nclc.org), and are quick to respond to these matters when contacted directly. Furthermore, they are in constant communication with the Department of Education and fight on behalf of student debtors on a daily basis in that arena, too.

Finally, this state-level solution relates directly to the last solution below, that of all American citizens getting actively engaged in the political process as well. The pressure to appeal to voters means something to state governors and other state executives. This is where voting, and other political forms of action such as protest, can become a powerful tool and one that can lead to results in solving the student loan debt crisis.

Actively support politicians who fight on behalf of student borrowers

We as voters play a role in whether American policy reflects intelligent long-term respect for higher education or short-sighted counterproductive thinking. This is where our votes at the ballot box matter. It is critical that anyone reading this book support political leaders who are compassionate towards people who have student loan debt and who understand the complexities that have led to the loan debt crisis. By recognizing the manipulations and inside deals that allowed many people to profit from student loans, we need to elect leaders who can propose and pass solutions like the ones I am proposing in this chapter. At this time, I suggest that political leaders like Senators Elizabeth

Warren (D-MA) and Sherrod Brown (D-OH) need our support, as they are some of the few voices on the Hill who genuinely care about the student loan debt crisis. Presidential Candidate Bernie Sanders is another leader who needs strong support.

The future of this problem will require ongoing discussion and investigation into which policymakers will support us and which are working against us. You can stay informed at my website *All Education Matters*. I will continue to track and provide information on key politicians, such as who is receiving donations from whom. Being familiar with the funds that go into campaigns, for example, is critical to recognizing which side a politician is on. Their donors influence the way they vote, the types of bills they introduce, and how they are swayed on issues. Knowing the politicians who are allied with us—whether you're a debtor, prospective student, current student, or the parent of a student or borrower—provides you the tools to help you make informed decisions when casting your ballot. Free membership at my website will offer you updates and information on these details, saving you the time on doing research on your own. By signing up, I ask you to join me in making the student debt crisis one of the highest priorities for our political leaders to solve.

Join me in taking action

While a debt jubilee would be a dream come true, I think most of us would agree it is unrealistic to expect this to happen. Nevertheless, it's still worth suggesting as a solution to discuss because there may be seeds of other ideas here. However, there are many other realistic and pragmatic solutions that could solve this problem. While we must look to policymakers to do the hard work that government must do to pass legislation to change the way the system works, every citizen is also empowered to get involved with this campaign for change.

If you have student loan debt, you already know that this problem is huge. You're living it every day, as is your family. No one needs to convince you that we're at a crisis level. Now consider that there are 43 million other Americans with student loan debt as well. Their stories are different, but collectively we are bound by one single cause: fixing the student loan debt crisis. Imagine what we could do together, if we joined forces to demand immediate change.

A well-regarded think tank, Demos, estimates that by 2025 outstanding student loan debt will hit $2 trillion. With each passing year, as graduates are handed their diplomas, they join our ranks. That is why we need to focus on the following actions:

- Support a presidential candidate who wants free public university education for all
- Become involved with state and federal government political leaders pushing for legislation that will allow us to refinance our student loans
- Push for solutions such as refinancing of student debt and making it possible to discharge federal and private loans in bankruptcy

We can choose to empower ourselves by getting informed and supporting political leaders who understand this issue. In so doing, these political leaders will be able to implement more policies that reflect compassion towards Americans who sought education to not only improve themselves individually but who seek to give back to their communities and to this nation.

Let's create an educated, informed, intelligent America.

End notes

1. To protect the identity of the sender, his name has been changed, and the brother-in-law's name as well as the university he and his wife attended have been redacted.

2. https://www.kansascityfed.org/publicat/reswkpap/pdf/rwp%2012-05.pdf

3. http://www.princetonmagazine.com/paul-krugman/

4. http://strikedebt.org/drom/chapter-four/

5. http://www.thecollegesolution.com/how-much-parents-and-students-are-borrowing-for-college/

6. http://blogs.wsj.com/economics/2015/05/08/congratulations-class-of-2015-youre-the-most-indebted-ever-for-now/

7. http://www.marketwatch.com/story/parents-youre-paying-for-college-wrong-2014-07-31

8. http://files.consumerfinance.gov/f/201207_cfpb_Reports_Private-Student-Loans.pdf

9. Sven Beckert, Katherine Stevens, and Students of the Harvard and Slavery Research Seminar (Harvard University Press, 2011), 7.

10. Suzanne Mettler, Soldiers to Citizens: The GI Bill and the Making of the Greatest Generation (Oxford University Press, 2007),

11. Ibid., 2

12. https://www.ida.org/~/media/Corporate/Files/Publications/STPIPubs/ida-d-3306.ashx

13. https://www.ida.org/~/media/Corporate/Files/Publications/STPIPubs/ida-d-3306.ashx

14. Source: http://www.jstor.org/stable/1033973?&seq=1#page_scan_tab_contents

15. http://www.jstor.org/stable/1033973?&seq=1#page_scan_tab_contents

16. Source: Jimmy Carter, Keeping Faith: Memoir of a President, University of Arkansas Press, 1995, 80

17. Carter's speech, October 17, 1979 (last accessed online, August 31, 2015, http://www.presidency.ucsb.edu/ws/?pid=31543).

18. http://www.salon.com/2013/03/09/the_world_according_to_milton_friedman_partner/

19. http://www.salon.com/2013/03/09/the_world_according_to_milton_friedman_partner/

20. http://www.ed.gov/news/press-releases/us-department-education-strengthens-federal-student-loan-servicing

21. Navient was formerly Sallie Mae, but when the company split in two in 2014, this became the new name for the side of the firm that handles servicing and asset recovery.

22. http://www.thecollegesolution.com/stunning-how-many-are-borrowing-for-college/

23. Consumer Financial Protection Bureau has been

investigating more of these private banks recently related to student loan servicing. There are only 10 student loan servicers, so if the findings are incriminating, this might lead to changes. Jury is out. http://www.wsj.com/articles/cfpb-investigating-wells-fargo-on-student-loan-servicing-1444333614

24. http://www.bloomberg.com/news/articles/2015-10-23/court-rules-that-student-loan-company-isn-t-above-the-law

25. http://www.inflation.eu/inflation-rates/united-states/historic-inflation/cpi-inflation-united-states-2015.aspx

26. http://www.huffingtonpost.com/2014/04/14/student-loan-profits_n_5149653.html

27. http://www.bloomberg.com/news/articles/2012-05-15/taxpayers-fund-454-000-pay-for-collector-chasing-student-loans

28. http://www.huffingtonpost.com/davidhalperin/new-forprofit-college-lob_b_1654224.html

29. http://www.huffingtonpost.com/davidhalperin/purveyors-of-wisdom-on-hi_b_8298242.html)

30. https://www.washingtonpost.com/opinions/bernie-sanders-america-needs-free-college-now/2015/10/22/a3d05512-7685-11e5-bc80-9091021aeb69_story.html

31. http://www.durbin.senate.gov/newsroom/press-releases/durbin-cohen-and-others-introduce-legislation-to-restore-fairness-in-student-lending

32. http://www.propublica.org/article/education-department-bureaucracy-keeps-disabled-borrowers-in-debt

33. http://college.usatoday.com/2011/06/21/illness-or-injury-can-cause-ruinous-consequences-for-those-with-student-loan-debt/

About the Author

 CRYN JOHANNSEN has been studying and covering the student loan crisis for many years. She received a B.A. with honors from the University of Kansas, an M.A. from the University of Chicago, and earned an M.A. at Brown University where she was in the PhD program and was an Exchange Scholar at Harvard University.

Based on her own challenges in repaying her student loan debt, she launched a blog, All Education Matters, (alleducationmatters.blogspot.com) to begin covering the crisis on behalf of millions of student debtors. Her blog is a non-profit, arguing for fair solutions and a new way to finance higher education for all Americans.

Cryn has made frequent trips to Washington, DC to meet with congressional leaders and their staff to discuss possible solutions that could be implemented to help current and distressed borrowers, a group of people who are underrepresented when it comes to policy issues that relate to higher education finance reform. Cryn has authored numerous articles about the student loan debt crisis for Huffington Post, The New England Journal of Higher Education, The Guardian, USA Today, Truthout.org, Money Crashers, and others. She has appeared on CNN, Headline News, RT News, and been interviewed by NPR, The Wall Street Journal Radio, among many other outlets.

More information can be found at alleducationmatters. blogspot.com. Cryn is available for radio and television interviews and to give speeches about the crisis.

If you enjoyed reading this book,
please share it with others on Facebook.

We'd also appreciate your review of it on
Amazon and on other book review websites.

66530103R00086

Made in the USA
Middletown, DE
06 September 2019